NORTH
AMERICA
from the best
AUTHORITIES.

THE AMERICAN REVOLUTION

As Described By British Writers
and
The Morning Chronicle and London Advertiser

Elizabeth R. Miller

HERITAGE BOOKS
2008

HERITAGE BOOKS
AN IMPRINT OF HERITAGE BOOKS, INC.

Books, CDs, and more—Worldwide

For our listing of thousands of titles see our website
at
www.HeritageBooks.com

Published 2008 by
HERITAGE BOOKS, INC.
Publishing Division
100 Railroad Ave. #104
Westminster, Maryland 21157

International Standard Book Numbers
Paperbound: 978-1-55613-466-1
Clothbound: 978-0-7884-7130-8

To LEW, My Devoted Husband,

With A Special Thank You

And All My Love

For

His Unending Support And Encouragement,

And Without Whose Technical Computer Assistance,

I Could Never Have Written This Book.

TABLE OF CONTENTS

PREFACE

Transatlantic Mail

When reading the *Morning Chronicle*, a British paper of the 1780s, it soon became apparent to me that the dispatches from North America during that time period frequently appeared outdated. A letter from New York to London may have traveled two to three months before publication. Even the correspondence from Paris, France, may not have reached London in less than ten days.

Curious about the mailing process of that era, I visited the Postal Museum in Bath, England. I found that even on the overland route from Liverpool to London, a distance of 210 miles (mileage on today's roads), a letter may have taken one week.

Stephen Howard, Assistant Curator of the Postal Museum, provided research which focused on the Post Office. The information for the research was obtained from a report produced by commissioners who were appointed to enquire into fees, gratuities, perquisites and emoluments in 1788. It seems that the speed of the old express post was six miles per hour which compared unfavorably with that of Palmer's mail-coaches, introduced on main roads between 1784 and 1786, which managed eight miles per hour.

In the Postal Museum Library, I found a book entitled *Transatlantic Mail* by Frank Staff (Harrap\Coles 1956). The following interesting paragraphs, excerpted with permission, provide the reader with some explanation regarding communication across the Atlantic during the Revolutionary War.

"The packets in service between Falmouth and New York were withdrawn from general Post Office duty and were refitted for war. They continued to carry mail, but no longer kept to any time-table. Their sailings were kept secret, and the public were informed of a departure only when a packet was bound for Halifax. From Halifax the mail was sent on to Boston or New York by first available ship."

"The Atlantic crossing was now beset with danger. American privateers, manned by men of finest caliber and of great daring, experiencing a new-found freedom, exulted in giving chase to the heavily laden British merchantmen on the West Indian run, and the English suffered heavy losses. The packet boats, too, were constantly being set upon, and the accounts of their engagements are many and glorious. Indeed, their fame reflected on their home port, so that the very name 'a Falmouth packet' came to be associated with bravery and achievement."

"Britain's plight became even more desperate when the Americans made an alliance with the French in 1778; the bravery and intrepid daring of these Falmouth packets is the more appreciated when it is considered how they ran the gauntlet across the Atlantic, hounded by both the Americans and the French. They fought back, always against heavy odds, and sometimes a packet made a capture of a vessel nearly twice its size. But their losses were great. Between the years 1779 and 1782, from those packets serving the North American ports, nine were captured and seven were seriously damaged. Five packets served New York, and of these four were captured and one was damaged; and of the three packets serving the Carolina station, two were taken."

"New York was recaptured by the British in 1776, and post offices were again established in other places under their control. During the period of this reoccupation, ships arrived with mail from Britain at Quebec and New York, but instead of being delivered to the local post-masters, the military authorities ordered it to be handed in to their headquarters, where officers were appointed to examine letters in efforts to find disloyal members of the community and to suppress information which might be useful to the enemy."

INTRODUCTION

A search for the true version of the American Revolutionary War has been attempted by many historians and writers on both sides of the Atlantic. How much is fiction and how much is fact? Undoubtedly, there are distorted views on both the American and British sides. Each country points to the enemy as the villain, while its own people represent the hero.

It, therefore, occurred to me to explore history books of the period written in England, and then research the British newspapers covering the last few years of that war.

British newspapers of the 1780s did not refer to what transpired as "The American Revolution." Unable to understand American dissatisfaction with British rule, they labeled the colonial resistance "The Rebellion."

Undoubtedly, journalists writing during that time reflected the mood and opinion of the British ministers and the British people. Opinions varied among Whigs and Tories. However, the general sentiment was that the colonists apparently enjoyed a rather high standard of living and refused to contribute a reasonable amount to the cost of their defense; in other words, it was simply a matter of tax evasion by British subjects, who defied British law on British territory.

It was not until the 20th century, that British historians realized and admitted that political and social changes in the colonies were largely responsible for the American Revolution, and therefore, "The Rebellion" was more than a struggle for independence.

Militarily speaking, it was and still is hard for the British to accept that the Americans succeeded in defeating one of the world's greatest powers. Undoubtedly, the British had several disadvantages; the biggest was the difficulty of deploying their troops across three thousand miles of ocean. Furthermore, the climate and the land of the American continent was unfamiliar to the British and many Americans were unfriendly. The support of the Loyalists was minute and contrary to expectations. Of course, military mistakes were made by the British, but most historians put the blame for England's defeat on France's entry into the war. France's entry on the side of the Americans forced Britain to fight on several fronts and at the same time, provided the Americans with financial aid, manpower and assistance at sea.

This book may not express historic precision, but it may shed some light on the struggles of the time and reveal to the reader the apprehensions, speculations and concerns of the British during that war.

(The newspaper articles used in this book were researched from the original papers, which are bound and available at the Bodleian Library in Oxford, England).

CHAPTER I

1764 - 1775

Laws and Issues that Provoked the Americans

During the 17th and 18th century, the American colonists gave their allegiance to the Crown, but at the same time showed an inclination to proceed along independent lines. Many Americans believed that Britain had lowered their status to that of slaves. They, therefore, realized the necessity of obtaining fundamental social, political and economic changes, which, in turn, required a struggle for independence.

The English, on the other hand, regarded the American colonists as fellow British subjects who did not conform to British law and who dared to take up arms against the militia of the king.

Fixed and distorted ideas on both sides of the Atlantic were, and still are, hard to overcome. National taboos are difficult to disregard.

In 1764, a writer in *The London Chronicle* insisted that "the colonies were acquired with no other view than to be a convenience to us, and therefore it can never be imagined that we are to consult their interest preferably to our own."[1] For the next twenty years, while the problem turned into a quarrel, the quarrel into a war and the war into a great national humiliation, this basic attitude continued to be held by most people in the home country. While "the colonists themselves might think in terms of right and wrong, freedom and tyranny, the British thought like shopkeepers, deciding whether or not to close down a branch that was losing money."[2]

The colonies were regarded as a source of raw materials (tar, sugar, tobacco, furs), and they also were the consumers of the goods manufactured in England. The majority of British laws were written for that purpose.

Ships that supported that trade were built in Britain, sailed by British seamen and managed and controlled by British merchants. Undoubtedly, an investment in this shipping enterprise resulted in great profits and created a powerful British fleet. The Navigation Laws then stipulated that all American goods from the colonies could be exported only in English or colonial ships, and had to be exported directly to England.

In 1722, England passed laws that forbade the export from the colonies of sugar, tobacco, cotton, ginger, wool, rice, copper, beaver skins and indigo to other foreign markets. Other laws precluded the import of goods coming directly from Europe to the colonies, and also limited any manufacture in the colonies that would compete with those in England, such as wool and iron.

British victories in the Seven Years' War (1756 to 1763), which ended with the Treaty of Paris, earned her enormous territories. France ceded to England all of her American holdings east of the Mississippi, (except the town of New Orleans, which was transferred to Spain). England now had gained extensive territory on the American continent and had more than doubled the land of the original colonies. In order to deter European powers from returning to places like Canada, populated by thousands of conquered French, Britain needed an army to police and govern the land. It was vital to employ several thousand troops, but the colonists did not want to provide these men, nor did they want to bear the burden of paying for them. In Britain, the national debt had doubled, due to the Seven Years' War, and it was thought only fair that the colonies should share the expense especially as they owed allegiance to England.

George Grenville, in 1764, proposed the Sugar Act and two other acts in order to secure more customs revenue, which previously did not even pay the cost of collection. However, only New England was affected by these laws. It was not until the Stamp Act in 1765 and the Townsend Acts in 1767, that the duties involved the other colonies. It was this taxation that caused the final rupture between the colonies and the Mother Country.

Why did the colonists object so vigorously? They assumed they were entitled to the same constitutional principles, the same rights and protections, and the same liberties as their brothers residing in England. If the English people could only be taxed with their consent, or the consent given by their representatives in Parliament on their behalf, the same rights should apply to the residents of America; otherwise, ministerial actions would be construed as an attempt to enslave them.

George Grenville became King George III's chief minister in 1763, at a time when the increased British Empire had penetrated the American continent and when the national debt was enormous. Although Grenville increased some British taxes, this was not enough to take care of the national debt and to administer and defend the colonies. Actually, the taxes imposed on the colonies were light compared to those paid by Britons at home. According to one estimate, "the average American paid a mere six pence a year, while the average Briton at home paid twenty-five shillings."[3]

The colonists had prospered during the Seven Years' War, but suffered a depression immediately afterwards. This hardship worsened with the Stamp Act of 1765, which taxed newspapers, legal documents, playing cards, insurance policies, etc. Not only did American merchants form non-importation associations to boycott the ordering and selling of British goods, but many attended a Stamp Act Congress in New York which emphasized that colonists could only be taxed by their own representative assemblies. Thus, the Stamp Act was a direct assertion of British authority.

The British government felt certain that "as long as the tax was on the statute book and enforced, so long would there be a symbol of colonial dependence upon the Mother Country. But if, as Grenville declared,

'Great Britain gives up her right of taxation, she gives up her right of sovereignty, which is inseparable from it in all ages and all countries'."[4]

By March of 1766, the English realized the blunder and, therefore, repealed the Stamp Act, after Grenville had been replaced by Lord Rockingham. However, Parliament passed a much more controversial law, the "Declaratory Act," which gave Parliament the right to make laws for the colonies in all cases whatsoever.

Although the Stamp Act failed, a new source of revenue in the colonies was sought by Charles Townsend, the new Chancellor of the Exchequer. His Revenue Act of 1767, imposed customs duties on the import of tea and several manufactured goods, such as glass, lead, paper and paint. The money raised by this act could be used for salaries paid to governors, judges and other royal officials who then would not have to depend on colonial assemblies. Also added was an American Board of Customs Commissioners at Boston, who were directly responsible to Britain.

Of course, the Americans objected again, saying that only colonial assemblies could tax them. Imported British goods were again boycotted. This led to disturbances and riots, such as the Boston Massacre.

In 1770, the Townsend measure of taxes was abandoned by Lord North, who headed a new British government, as the measure actually cost more money than it brought in. Yet, not all duties were repealed. The customs duty on tea was retained, which was to emphasize to the colonists the continuing supremacy of Parliament.

King George III insisted, "I do not wish to come to severer measures, but we must not retreat; by coolness and an unremitted pursuit of the measures that have been adopted, I trust they will come to submit; I have no objection afterwards to their seeing that there is no indication for the present to lay fresh taxes on them, but I am clear there must always be one tax to keep up the right, and as such I approve of the Tea Duty."[5]

The colonists refused to buy British tea and frequently smuggled in Dutch tea. Lord North then enacted the Tea Act of 1773, whereby, the East India Company (which was at the brink of bankruptcy) could sell tea directly to America. Although this made tea cheaper, the Townsend duty still had to be paid. The colonists looked at this procedure as another way to demand revenue and also to restrict their trade. Eventually this led to the famous Boston Tea Party in December 1773, when tea was dumped into Boston Harbor.

Britain, and specifically Parliament and the North Ministry, had to retaliate and punish Boston for destroying 50,000 dollars worth of private property. The Coercive Acts of 1774 closed the Boston port and also empowered the governor of Massachusetts to make all appointments for judges, sheriffs and magistrates, and it disallowed all town meetings. At this time, General Thomas Gage, the commander-in-chief in America, was appointed as the new governor of Massachusetts, giving every indication of making it a military rule.

It was King George III who was strongly opposed to conciliation. "I am not apt to be oversanguine; but I cannot help being of the opinion that with firmness and perseverance America will be brought to submission."[6]

3

General Gates, however, sized up the situation very well when he wrote from New York: "Surely the people of England can never be such dupes to believe the Americans have traded with them so long out of pure love and brotherly affection. That they will manufacture, when they are able, is easy to conceive, in spite of your laws to prevent them, but this is looking into futurity. That they will struggle for independency, if the good folks at home are not already convinced of it, they will soon be convinced. From denying the right of internal taxation, they next deny the right of duty upon imports and thus they mean to go on step by step till they throw off all subjection to your laws."[7]

General Gates also pinpointed colonial sentiments. He wrote that there are "three fundamentals on which the people of this country endeavor to establish the political doctrines they have promulgated, and as they fail in producing proof from the one, have recourse to the other. These are Charter Rights, British Constitution, and the Laws of God and Nature."[8]

The colonists believed that the British were taking away their liberties, and with sympathy for Massachusetts, resistance spread to the other colonies. Eventually, this led to the meeting of the Continental Congress in September 1774, which absolutely refused the idea that the colonies were under the authority of Parliament and emphasized that only American legislatures could stipulate taxation.

CHAPTER II

1775 - 1780

Various Battles and Historical Events
as Seen by British Writers

In April of 1775, hostilities led to the skirmishes at Lexington and Concord. When the Continental Congress met in May, many of the representatives still hoped that differences between the colonies and the Mother Country could be resolved, which would leave Americans loyal to the King. However, the Massachusetts confrontations provoked the residents of the other colonies and many prepared for war.

That same month, Ethan Allen and his Vermonters (the British called them "rebels") conquered Fort Ticonderoga on Lake Champlain. Then, in June of 1775, General Gage, while trying to defend Boston from the Massachusetts Militia, won the Battle of Bunker Hill with a high cost of British casualties.

Meanwhile, Congress had made plans to raise a Continental Army and appointed George Washington as commander-in-chief.

In August, King George III proclaimed that the American colonies were in a state of rebellion. He said: "The dye is now cast, the colonies must either submit or triumph."[1]

Military clashes continued. The American colonists became convinced that independence was a necessity though they fully realized that this could only be obtained by war. Encouraged by the battles of Lexington, Concord and Bunker Hill, the spirit of rebellion was aroused and brought about resistance against all kinds of British rule and military actions.

In October 1775 while General Washington was besieging Boston, General Thomas Gage, the military governor of Massachusetts, resigned and was replaced by Sir William Howe. The latter was hoping for additional help from England. The British government sent troops under the leadership of Sir Henry Clinton; however, he was dispatched to North and South Carolina, where southern loyalists were to join him. Without the much needed support, Boston could not be defended, and the British had to evacuate Boston in March of 1776. Sir William Howe took his troops to Nova Scotia. In the South, the loyalists did not lend the anticipated support, and Sir Henry Clinton and his troops sailed toward home.[+] It was obvious that the British did not accomplish the projected isolation of the rebellion in Massachusetts, and the ministry was disappointed in the expected loyalist support.

There was no united front among the British ministers and the King. "A King anxious to reassert dominion over as many provinces as possible in the shortest time, Sandwich (4th Earl) pessimistic about the navy, Barrington (Viscount) all for a naval war, Weymouth (3rd Viscount) eager to make New England smart for its sedition, Lord North wielding a sword in one hand, while still clutching an olive branch in the other, the Ministers were sufficiently distracted."[3]

On July 4, 1776, Congress adopted the Declaration of Independence, which was the only way to give Americans the liberties they wanted.

In September of that year, the British captured New York after defeating George Washington at the Battle of Long Island. It was General Howe's plan that by occupying New York, New England could be cut off. General Washington had to retreat across New Jersey and moved into Pennsylvania. However, by the end of December, Washington returned across the Delaware and was victorious at Trenton.

In January 1777, Washington defeated the British at Princeton, and in April of that year, the Marquis de La Fayette, with French volunteers, landed in the Carolinas to assist the colonists in their fight for freedom.

Britain's next plan, based on advice by General Burgoyne, was to have British troops under Burgoyne "move from Canada southward upon Albany, at the head of navigation on the Hudson; Howe's army in New York was to move northward up the Hudson to Albany...Full instructions were sent from London to the Canadian authorities to launch the northern half of the joint expedition. But no definite instructions were sent to Howe, who moved against Philadelphia instead of Albany...The British had large forces in Canada and a strong army in New York under Howe. Had these troops been concentrated at New York, the Crown could have put 35,000 strongly equipped regulars in the field. If an energetic British commander had then used them to strike relentlessly at Washington's little army of 8,000 Continentals in New Jersey, the revolt would almost certainly have been crushed."[4]

The failure of General Burgoyne's plan and the anticipated destruction of Washington's army apparently could be blamed on "Lord George Germain, who directed military operations in America. He dictated a letter, which would have caused General Howe to move northward from New York to meet General Burgoyne advancing from Canada. Germaine went off to the country without waiting to sign the letter; it was mislaid among other papers; Howe was without needed instructions; and the disaster followed."[5]

+ Lord George Germain, who had become Secretary of the colonies in December of 1775, had convinced the ministry of the loyalists' support. "An extreme contempt for the rebels caused him to swallow over-readily tales of loyalists waiting only the lead and opportunity to declare for King George. This fiction, lovingly embraced by the American Secretary, proved more damaging to British strategy."[2]

Howe succeeded in taking Philadelphia in September of 1777, but he was unsuccessful in destroying George Washington's army.

However, the British troops moving toward New England from Canada were having major problems. Although they took Fort Ticonderoga from the Americans, the rebels hindered their advances by blocking roads and destroying bridges. In fact, the troops from Lake Ontario did not make it to Albany and that left General Burgoyne's army unprotected and its supply line cut off. "Sometimes his men were without food and equipment...he was dependent on his communications for every form of supplies...The perennial problem for the British in all operations was this one of food."[6]

General Gates and his American forces blocked Burgoyne's southward move toward Albany, and a New England militia attacked the British from the East. When General Burgoyne was surrounded, he capitulated at Saratoga the 19th of October 1777. Thus, Britain's Canadian army was wiped out and the Britons' anticipated victory had turned into a major defeat.

Burgoyne was "a gallant soldier; but he was vain, boastful and superficial, and not a man to depend upon in a tight corner. The very successes of the beginning of the expedition caused him further to enmesh himself in the deadly snare. When the situation had obviously become impossible, he pretended that his orders forbade him to retire, as if the orders to a general can ever compel the impossible. When at last he reconciled himself to submission to fate and ordered a retreat, it was too late. The unfortunate general and his army were surrounded."[7]

Anyone watching the British military movements at that time "might think that madness had seized the British leaders; Burgoyne on the upper Hudson plunging forward resolutely to meet Howe; Howe at sea sailing away, as it might well seem, to get as far from Burgoyne as he could; Clinton in command at New York without instructions, puzzled what to do and not hearing from his leader, Howe, for six weeks at a time; and across the sea a complacent minister, Germain, who believed that he knew what to do in a scene three thousand miles away and had drawn up exact instructions as to the way of doing it, and who was now eagerly awaiting news of the final triumph."[8]

The capitulation of the British at Saratoga was a decisive factor for France. Although the French had been sympathetic to the American struggle for freedom and had given secret help to the American colonies, an open alliance had not yet been planned. French aid had been sought by the colonists since 1776, when Silas Deane, a member of the Continental Congress, was named envoy to France. By the end of that year, Benjamin Franklin was sent to Paris and Arthur Lee was named the third member of the Commission.

Besides sending goods and arms to the American colonists, France was persuaded by Benjamin Franklin to grant the colonists a no-interest loan of two million dollars which did not have to be repaid until America recovered from the war. In time, France followed up with other loans which added up to about 26 million francs.

After Burgoyne's defeat, France was ready on February 6, 1778, to sign a treaty of Commerce and Friendship with America, which also gave her the opportunity to seek vengeance for having been humiliated by the British at the end of the Seven Year War.

While in Paris, both Deane and Franklin were approached by British agents, who offered them "a safe conduct to London, permanent places in the American nobility, which the Government proposed to create in the colonies, and an immediate armistice in the war."[9]

The offers of conciliation made in March, after the French entry into the war, allowed "equal participation in the benefit of the British constitution with the virtual concession of Home Rule, and a new political organization even on terms laid down by the Americans. There were to be Treaties for the suspension of arms, and for the establishment of peace, friendship and commerce."[10]

However, after careful perusal of the British offers, "Franklin now found from the propositions, that the ministers cannot yet divest themselves of the idea that the power of Parliament over us is constitutionally absolute and unlimited; and that the limitations they may be willing now to put to it by treaty are so many favours, or so many benefits, for which we are to make compensation...Franklin did not, therefore, accept these terms...but admitted the propositions probably would have been accepted if they had been made two years ago. I have answered that they have come too late."[11]

Also in February 1778, General Howe's resignation was approved by Lord Germain, and he returned to England. His command in America was taken over by Sir Henry Clinton.

Shortly after France entered the war, King George III "made an acute analysis of the strategic situation...He wrote to North that should a French war now be our fate, the only means of making such a war successful would be the withdrawal of the greatest part of the troops from America, and employing them against the French and Spanish settlements, for if we were to carry on both a land war against the rebels, and also contend with France and Spain, it must be feeble in all parts and consequently unsuccessful."

The King also suggested that Lord North bring his new American peace propositions to Parliament. "North introduced his motions on February 17th - to renounce all claim to taxation and to empower Commissioners to treat with any persons or bodies of men in America for peace."[12]

On April 24, 1778, a British peace commission sailed for America headed by Lord Carlisle, which arrived in Philadelphia on June 6th. However, the King did not "think fit to slacken any preparations which had been judged necessary for the carrying on of the war - it being His Majesty's firm purpose to prosecute it with the utmost vigor, in case the colonies shall obstinately persist in their refusal to return to their allegiance and pay obedience to the constitutional authority of the Government."[13]

The Peace Commission was instructed "you are not to decline entering into consideration of the said proposal so long as the sovereignty of the Mother Country was not infringed, or powers given to such Congress as would imperil the sovereign rights of the Crown and the constitutional control of Great Britain."[14]

The Peace Commission, which arrived at a time when British troops were retreating, failed in their negotiations with Congress and in July asked permission to return home.

With France entering the war, Britain had to use some of their troops stationed in America and send them to fight the French in the West Indies. This gave the American colonists a chance to regain Philadelphia in June, while the British evacuated that city and retreated northward to Sandyhook from where they were taken by the fleet to New York. At about the same time, Compte D'Estaing's French fleet arrived at the coast of Virginia. The French navy commander apparently had hoped to surprise the British at Philadelphia and to wipe out their fleet and capture their army. It seems that the weather thwarted his plans and helped the British out of a difficult situation.

Now the focus of the war in America shifted to the south where loyalism to the King was supposed to be still strong. In December 1778, British troops occupied Savannah, Georgia, and later won control of Georgia.

In June of 1779, Spain also entered the war on the American side and the siege of Gibraltar began. By August, the British were in serious trouble as the French fleet occupied the channel, threatening invasion. However, on American soil, British troops repulsed a French-American siege of Savannah, ending in the retreat of the rebels.

CHAPTER III

January - October 1780

From
The Morning Chronicle and London Advertiser
(unless otherwise noted)

(All quotations, except headings)

IS GEORGE WASHINGTON DEAD?
READY FOR A NEW PEACE TREATY?
January 17, 1780

Extract from a letter from Paris, January 4.
   A French frigate arrived at Brest the 30th of December in 24 days from Boston, giving an account of the following interesting intelligence, and which seems to gain credit every hour, the truth of which is much dreaded here, that Washington, who had been ill for some time past, died at Philadelphia the 27th of November at one o'clock in the morning, in consequence thereof there was a confused meeting of the Congress, which they were obliged to adjourn to the day following, on account of the riotous disposition of the people. When the members met, it was resolved, in order to appease the minds of the people, they would now seriously think of peace with Great Britain on these terms: That the King should give up one of the younger branches of his Royal Family to be elected Supreme Prince of the American empire and to form a lasting alliance, offensive and defensive, as also several laws with regard to trade and commerce, for the mutual advantage of both nations, and that their allies should be included in the aforesaid treaty, when every advantage and disadvantage is to remain in the same state as at the beginning of the articles. Let it be as it will, Franklin has since had pretended honours paid him, which is believed he would rather dispense with, namely, guards, or rather spies, for fear he should withdraw to Holland.

HELP THE LOYALISTS WHO RETURNED TO ENGLAND!
January 24, 1780

To the Lords Commissioners of His Majesty's Treasury:
   In the beginning of the rebellion they judged it impossible that this country could have been so inhospitable, or the people so barbarous as to deny them their charitable protection. Humanity is wounded by the

treatment they receive; their attachment to this country is their disgrace and they are held in derision for all they have lost and endured; here much have they to deplore and the frenzy of the times, when they find men that would applaud them had they bowed to the shrine of the despotic Congress and suffered their fears to have given an apology for their treachery, - this had been meritorious! But they preferred every distress to the forfeiture of their allegiance; they have withstood all the threats of the usurped authority; they despised all the rebellious laws and though many of their unhappy friends and neighbors have fallen victims to Congressional cruelty - cruelty countenanced by their legislatures! Yet they have withstood them all!

It is to your Lordships that these unhappy men appeal for saccour. Many are now in this city groaning under every want, because they are destitute of powerful friends, therefore their petitions long unnoticed. - Cruel Partiality - are they not equally entitled to your Lordships' care and protection?

AMERICA NEEDS FINANCIAL HELP!
February 4, 1780

All the late accounts of America, as well by way of New York as that of St. Eustatia, agree that the Congress are, to use a vulgar phrase, got to the length of their tether; they cannot carry on the war with a less sum in hard dollars than 800,000! But have not the means of raising an 8th part of it. They are disappointed in all their promises they receive from France and Spain, and General Washington has written repeatedly to them, that without remittances it is impossible to keep his little army together, though it amounts to no more than 6,000 men. This has induced them to send Messrs. Laurens and Adams to Europe, in hopes they will receive fresh offers from Great Britain.

ASSEMBLY IN PENNSYLVANIA - A GOVERNMENT OF VILLAINS
February 11, 1780

Dated New York, December 2.

The Pennsylvania Gazette of the 17th ult. contains an act of the newfangled assembly of that province for vesting the estates of the late proprietaries of Pennsylvania in their imaginary commonwealth.

It is not a little surprising that a set of men, who have had address enough to set great part of Europe in a ferment, should so soon discover principles, which must place them in the first rank of the most detestable villains that ever encumbered any part of the globe.

REPORT ON FRENCH TROOP MOVEMENT FROM THE GENERAL ADVERTISER & MORNING INTELLIGENCER
March 14, 1780

By Saturday's Holland, French & Flanders mail.

The Marquis de la Fayette had his audience of leave of his Majesty at Versailles the 29th of last month; on his return to America, where he is to serve under the Count de Rochambault, who goes out with eight regiments to the assistance of the United States.

REPORT ON FRENCH NAVY
April 17, 1780

Extract from a letter from Paris, April 3.
Seven ships of the squadron destined for America are in the road, but the expedition is kept as great a mystery as possible. It is not yet known of what number of ships the squadron will be composed, nor will it ever be known when they will sail for Brest, as fifteen or eighteen ships may go at once.

CLINTON REQUESTS MEN FOR HIS ATTACK ON CHARLESTON
May 5, 1780

It is said, dispatches have been received from New York since the receipt of Sir Henry Clinton's last letters, which mention that Sir Henry is now arrived with his army within fighting distance of Charlestown; that they were employed in erecting batteries against the town and that an experiment had already been made of the bomb ketches, and other instruments of devastation, which were near enough to reach the town. Sir Henry has sent to General Robertson, the Governor of New York, and commander of the forces there in Sir Henry's absence, for a reinforcement of 3,000 men, the enemy being better provided for resistance than was originally supposed.

PAUL JONES SEEN IN PARIS
May 10, 1780

Extract of a letter from Paris, April 13.
The famous Paul Jones, actually lodges in this city with Mr. Adams, at the Hotel de Valois, Rue de Richelieu. Last Tuesday he went to the Opera, where he received the applause of the audience, who testified their joy to see that intrepid mariner.

CLINTON RETURNS TO NEW YORK, LEAVING CORNWALLIS IN CHARLESTON.
RUMORS OF AMERICAN CAMPAIGN
June 17, 1780

General Clinton before the packet sailed from Charlestown, was gone to New York with a great part of the troops, and had left Lord Cornwallis with 5,000 men in possession of the city.
Extraordinary as it may appear, we are assured, that the officer, who was charged with the last Government dispatches from Admiral Arbutnot, declared in the drawingroom at St. James' on Thursday, that an American officer, of the name of Scott, who was made prisoner at the capture of Charlestown, told him that Congress had with the utmost difficulty prevailed on the Americans to support the expense and inconvenience of the present campaign, and that the chief reason which

induced them to enter upon it, was a confident assertion that the cities of London and Westminster would be laid in ashes this summer.

LETTER FROM CLINTON TO LORD GERMAIN, DESCRIBING THE SURRENDER OF CHARLESTON AND LOYALIST SUPPORT THERE
July 6, 1780

From *The General Advertiser & Morning Intelligencer.*
The following letters from Sir Henry Clinton, Knight of the Bath, Commander in Chief of His Majesty's forces in North America, to the Right Hon. Lord George Germain, one of his Majesty's principal Secretaries of State, were this day received by Lt. Col. Bruce, one of Sir Henry Clinton's Aids du Camp, who arrived in the South Carolina packet.

Headquarters, Charlestown, South Carolina, June 4, 1780.
I had the honor in my dispatch, No. 88, by the Earl of Lincoln, to communicate to your Lordship the surrender of Charlestown...
I informed your Lordship, that Lt. Gen. Earl Cornwallis was to march up the North side of Santee, whilst another corps moved up the hither shore of that river, towards the district of ninety-six. These corps are in motion, as well as one up the Savannah river in Georgia.
The troops immediately under his Lordship's command have pressed so effectually upon a body of the Rebels, which remained in the Province, that the Earl by detaching his corps of cavalry, and with them the legion infantry (mounted) has completed the destruction of everything in arms against us in this Province.
Lt. Col. Tarleton headed this detachment, whose celerity in performing a march of near a hundred miles in two days, was equal to the ardour with which they attacked the enemy. These refusing the terms which were offered them, were charged, and defeated with the loss of 172 killed and some taken, together with the remaining field artillery of the Southern army, their colours and baggage.
With the greatest pleasure I further report to your Lordship, that the inhabitants from every quarter repair to the detachment of the army, and to this garrison, to declare their allegiance to the King, and to offer their services, in arms, in support of his government. In many instances they have brought prisoners, their former oppressors or leaders; and I may venture to assert that there are few men in South Carolina, who are not either our prisoners, or in arms with us.
I have also the satisfaction to receive correspondence accounts that the loyalists in the back parts of North Carolina are arming. I dare entertain hopes that Lord Cornwallis's presence on that frontier, and perhaps within the province, will call back its inhabitants from their state of error and disobedience. If a proper naval force can be collected, I purpose sending a small expedition into Cape Fear river, to favor the revolution I look for higher in the country.
I am with the troops I could take, quitting the harbour of Charlestown, on my way to New York, hoping no foreign armament can yet have reached the coast, or have been able to attempt anything in our absence against that place.

H. Clinton

CLINTON SENDS GERMAIN COPIES OF TWO PROCLAMATIONS
REGARDING LOYALISTS, REBELS, PRISONERS AND PARDONS
July 10, 1780

Dated Headquarters, Charlestown, June 3, 1780.
I have the honour to enclose for your Lordship's information, the copies of two proclamations I have found it necessary to issue as Commander in Chief.

PROCLAMATION

Whereas notwithstanding the gracious offers which have been made to receive to his Majesty's peace and protection, with pardon and oblivion for their past offenses, all those his deluded and infatuated subjects who should return to their duty and a due obedience to the laws; yet there are some wicked and desperate men, who, regardless of the ruin and misery in which the country will be involved, are still endeavouring to support the flame of rebellion, and, under pretense of authority derived from the late usurped legislatures, are attempting by enormous fines, grievous imprisonments, and sanguinary punishments, to compel his Majesty's faithful and unwilling subjects to take up arms against his authority and government; and it is therefore become necessary, as well for the protection of the loyal subjects, as to procure the establishment of peace and good government in the country, to prevent, by the terror of example, such enormous offenses being committed in future; I have therefore thought fit to issue this my Proclamation to declare, that if any person shall hereafter appear in arms in order to prevent the establishment of his Majesty's Government in this country, or shall, under any pretense or authority whatsoever, attempt to compel any other person or persons to do so, or who shall hinder or intimidate, or attempt to hinder or intimidate, the King's faithful and loyal subjects from joining his forces, or otherwise performing those duties their allegiance requires, such person or persons to offending shall be treated with that severity so hardened and criminal an obstinacy will deserve, and his or their estates will be immediately seized in order to be confiscated. And for the encouragement of the King's faithful and peaceable subjects, I do again assure them, that they shall meet with effectual countenance; and whatever the situation of the country will permit of the restoration of Civil Government and peace, they will by the Commissioners appointed by his Majesty for that purpose, be restored to the full possession of that liberty in their persons and property, which they had before experienced under the British Government. And that so desirable an event may be the more speedily accomplished, I do hereby, in his Majesty's name, require and command all persons whatever to be aiding and assisting to his forces whenever they shall be required, in order to extipate the rebellion, and thereby restore peace and prosperity to this, at present desolated and distracted country.
H. Clinton

PROCLAMATION

Whereas after the arrival of his Majesty's forces under my command in this Province in February last, numbers of persons were made prison-

15

ers by the army, or voluntarily surrendered themselves as such, and such persons were afterwards dismissed on their respective paroles; And whereas since the surrender of Charlestown, and the defeats and dispersion of the Rebel forces, it becomes unnecessary that such paroles should be any longer observed; and it is fit and proper that all persons should take an active part in settling and securing his Majesty's Government, and delivering the country from that anarchy, which for some time past has prevailed; I do therefore issue this my proclamation, to declare that all the inhabitants of the province, who are now prisoners upon parole, and were not in the military line (those who were in Fort Moultrie and Charlestown at the times of their capitulation and surrender, or were then in actual confinement, excepted) that from and after the 20th day of June instant, they are freed and exempted from all such paroles, and may hold themselves as restored to all the rights and duties belonging to citizens and inhabitants. And all persons under the description before mentioned, who shall afterwards neglect to return to their allegiance, and to his Majesty's Government, will be considered as enemies and rebels to the same, and treated accordingly.

H. Clinton

CLINTON ARRIVES IN NEW YORK
July 31, 1780

New York, June 21.

Last Saturday evening the inhabitants of this city were made supremely happy by the late arrival of his Excellency, General Sir Henry Clinton, from the conquest and complete reduction of South Carolina; his Excellency having restored peace and perfect decorum amongst the inhabitants of that opulent populous and very important Colony.

WASHINGTON'S LETTER TO HANCOCK, WRITTEN AFTER THE LOSS OF CHARLESTON
August 9, 1780

(A morning paper says the public may depend on the truth of what follows. It is sent by a correspondent, whose connection in America gives him every opportunity of knowing what passes in Congress).

You are to inform Congress that I received the honour of their letter of the 16th, but that my resolution if not fixed finally before, is now in fact determined. The surrender of Charlestown explains every doubt.

Tell them, Sir, that whilst I was supported with even the most distant prospect of success, my life and all I hold dear was at their service. Tell them I acted from no mean views - from no private purpose. My sentiments were open and candid, as they were constantly delivered. I said I would hold my services to my country, a duty, whilst there were uprightness in the cause and unanimity in the people; sorry am I now to say that tyranny is substituted for freedom in the magistrate, and that defection outsoars a love of virtuous liberty in all our troops. I am therefore no longer the commanding officer of the brave citizens struggling for their rights; I am only a distressed superior among dissatisfied, disaffected complainants, whose ardour is cooled, and whose native virtue no

16

longer exists. My troops are tired of war, and destitute of the common comforts of a soldier. I tremble for them when the dreadful day of final decision comes on; when they must (for now it is not to be postponed or avoided) meet an army flushed with victory and refreshed with all the necessaries of war. Tell Congress all these things, and say I entreat them to reconsider my former letter, and as they love the peace and future happiness of poor America, to offer an unconditional sheath to the British sword. Generous even in the hour of their bitterest anger, we need not dread the terms that the English may inflict. It is their interest now to seek our amity as well as our subjection.

Our friends in London are no longer considered the friends of the people. The faction is split; and for one wellwisher we had in England, we have now a hundred enemies. Indeed, and I speak it from the bottom of my heart, we were all along deceived both by Mr. B. and his party. We never had the love of the English since we took up arms - it was only the pernicious views of faction there that misrepresented matters here. But this is not a time to prove the cursed cause of the present state of affairs.

In the name of God, I then conjure them to give up the contest, and seek in an humble submission that peace which our arms can never restore. We may again be reinstated in tranquility, and whilst we mourn the relative slain, we will pray that in their deaths all animosity with England may forever by buried. The thoughts of the people will soon be turned to industry; and as our enmity with Great Britain would close the scene of war with France and Spain, the ports of Europe would again be opened. Do, Sir, represent these matters, and, in my name, desire that the last letter I sent may again be referred to. It contains such truths, relative to the state of our credit, and the impossibility of carrying on the war, as must convince, if seriously attended to.

I pray God to direct the resolves of Congress for the best; and that they may with my eyes see inevitable destruction to America, in a shameful and total overthrow of her army, if the voice of peace does not immediately stop the victorious troops of Clinton.

G. Washington

(The following is said to be a genuine copy of Mr. Hancock's answer to General Washington's letter):

I received your two letters; and that your sentiments might be as fully conveyed to Congress as they are to me, I sent copies of both to each member, which, as the subject was of such a nature as to make its general publication dangerous to the States, we had a private meeting to consider of.

After recapitulating your conduct since you were vested with command, and minutely examining the motives that induced you to take up arms in defense of your country, we must readily acquit you of any sinister design, or any treasonable intention. You have as a General, acted with a prudent caution, and avoided any decisive action with the enemy. This undoubtedly was our original plan; and you have well executed it. If there were any opportunities which might have gained an advantage for the army of the States, and which offered themselves in that want of Generalship so evident in the late British General (and palpably so from the inactive state of his troops, and the extraordinary

17

movements he made) such opportunities in being omitted, are not chargeable to your account; We recollect the strict injunctions you had, not to risque a battle, and we console ourselves in the loss of a few advantages by your many escapes from danger, when an attack by the enemy might have finally put an end to all our hopes. These escapes, Sir, we attribute as well to your military skill, as to the hand of Providence in choosing Ministers for the British King, that were unacquainted with the merits and demerits of their own officers.

Hitherto we have been favored with many marks of Providence in our favour. We have now the assistance of two great allies, from whose interposition, we had but very faint hopes at the beginning of the war. Those nations have taken a decided part in our favour; and as it was the world's opinion, that in the last war between the House of Bourbon and the House of Hanover, America was the ally that turned the scale in favour of Great Britain, so are we now to hope that she will preponderate with equal weight on the side of France and Spain. To talk therefore of making submission, is to talk idly. We are now a match for our haughty enemy; they know it, they dread it, and the language of their patriots speaks it.

You say that our finances are low, and our paper money not current; that the troops are discontented and in some parts almost famishing. You likewise tell us of innumerable desertions, and that the disaffected are many. All these, Mr. Washington, may be true, and it is what we are to expect; But Great Britain herself has disaffected men in her army, her navy and her senate. We have convincing proofs every day, of a kindling rebellion in the very heart of that proud empire; and we have the strongest reason to say that in a very short time you will hear of the entire destruction of her capital. Like ancient Rome, her guards are sunk into luxury; and when the day of trial comes, you will find, those who boast of Majesty will shrink from obedience, and be either silent spectators of the tumult, or else join the revolution. Trust me, Mr. Washington, Heaven has great things yet in store for us; and with such a prospect, it is blasphemy against the cause we fight in, to utter a distrust of Providence. As to our credit being low - so is that of England. Our paper currency, is as good as their stocks. The value of either is ideal, and the only difference lies in long custom, having established English faith, and want of time, to prove American punctuality, having raised suspicions of our honesty. We should therefore, by every stratagem, keep up the spirits of the people, their despondence alone can do credit an injury.

Disaffection is dangerous, and therefore, by severity in punishment, should be stopped. A few examples always deter the herd; and, if you practice, you will find good consequences in the advice. As to deserters, if they do not go over to the enemy, it is only an inconvenience pro tempore. We generally get them again either as recruits, or by proclamation of pardon. But, Sir, you surprise us in saying, the troops are famished. The rate of provision is regularly paid for and our contractors are honest men. There surely must be some mistake in that part of your letter, or the complaints made to you are without foundation. However, an enquiry into that supposed grievance shall instantly be made, and I can pledge myself to you, in the name of Congress, that the cause, if any, shall be immediately done away.

18

The last dispatch we had from Dr. Franklin, speaks highly of the honorable mention in which the army under your command, is made throughout the French dominions; and he gives us every assurance, that so soon as the Channel fleet of Britain is blocked up in Portsmouth, and that Rodney is defeated in the West Indies, a reinforcement both of men and money will be sent to America. The great superiority of the House of Bourbon at sea, gives them an authority to talk in high terms of doing as they please with the British fleet. Indeed, the navy of England cannot thrive so fast now, as it did last war; for every difficulty that the ingenious devices of the opposition there can form, is daily practiced to prevent the First Lord of the Admiralty from doing his business. Not that this is done more to serve us, than it is from the avowed hatred which the patriots bear that Noble man; an hatred, which will never cease, as it arises from the strong passion jealousy. We may therefore hope, in a short time, to see the fleet of England moulder away - and then, without any internal commotion, her fun of glory is set forever.

The melancholy contour of your letter has much affected us all. We know your abilities and have a strong confidence in them; you are loved and adored by the army; and even your enemies allow you merit. If you desert us, it may do us essential mischief. The English consider you as our sheet-anchor; and your resignation would indeed be a triumph to them. You must not therefore, at this time, think of it. The very idea is dangerous, and if published, would sow discontent indeed through the army. Lucrative motives, we are certain, are no object to you, or you might name your terms. The gratitude of America, is, however, superior to the promises of Congress, and when the day of peace comes, her glorious General will not be forgot.

As to the conquest of Charlestown, it is indeed an immense loss to us; but the victory of Britain in Carolina, will be short-lived; we have friends who are working such a mine, as will blow up all their triumphal schemes; and if Providence favours us, the news of the surrender will come to their ears a day too late for their rejoicing in London. I have already given you a hint that must raise your expectation - the explanation will surprise you. (Here follow about twenty lines of strange figures, somewhat like Hebrew characters, explanatory no doubt of the intended fire in London).

In a steadfast hope that the god of Battles will direct you how best to act, should Clinton attack you.

J. Hancock

SOME PARTICULARS OF THE LIFE OF MR. HENRY LAURENS, LATE PRESIDENT OF THE AMERICAN CONGRESS - NOW A PRISONER IN ENGLAND
October 9, 1780

When the ministry attempted to enforce the Stamp Act in America, Mr. Laurens drew upon himself the hatred of the populace of Charlestown by declaring their opposition to the act to be illegal and unconstitutional. They threatened him with the effects of their resentment, but were afterwards induced by persuasion to leave him unmolested. The repeal of the Stamp Act soon followed, and the animosities to which it had given rise, either disappeared, or for a while lay dormant. But success had now emboldened the Americans; it had enlarged their views and ambitions and made them look forward to new and distant triumphs. They demanded a repeal of the duties on glass, paints, etc. and threatened they would import no goods from this country if they were refused. They were refused, and they accordingly embraced the non-importation scheme. Mr. Laurens at first showed himself averse to this measure; but when he saw that the different colonies were no longer to try their several strengths by separate contests with the mother country, but were to concentrate their scattered powers by forming a General Congress, he eagerly entered into a scheme, which he had formerly reprobated. Such stability was now given to the proceedings of the factious colonies, that even a man of Mr. Laurens's prudence and wariness thought it no longer unsafe to strengthen them by his approbation and concurrence. In this, as in the former struggle, the American came off victorious.

When things began to assume a more settled appearance after the none-importation agreement was annulled, Mr. Laurens left Carolina, and came over to Europe. He remained about three years out of America, the greatest part of which he spent in England. In the beginning of 1775 he returned to Charlestown in time enough to fan the kindling flame of rebellion. His wealth, his knowledge of trade, his well-known industry and affiduity in every scheme he entered into, and the information he had acquired from his residency in England, rendered him a most valuable acquisition to the American cause, and marked him out as the most proper person the Carolinians could elect to be president of their provincial Congress. But even here his habitual caution, and even cunning, were not laid aside; for not withstanding the decisive part which his actions demonstrated he had taken in the grand dispute, he still pretended to the Loyalists that he was averse to the measures which the Americans were pursuing, and that for his part he was absolutely forced into them by his countrymen. He dreaded the vengeance of Britain if he should prove successful, and thought to elude it by this shallow artifice.

From this period the history of Mr. Laurens became an object of the attention of Europe, and is accordingly contained in all the prints of the time. It will be therefore sufficient to say, that soon after his being chosen President of the Provincial Congress of Carolina, he was sent as a delegate from the province to the Continental Congress at Philadelphia, that in 1777 he was elected President of the Continental Congress; and that while he was President, the infamous convention at Saratoga was entered into between Gates and Burgoyne. These things are yet recent; and the nation, moreover still boils with indignation at American treachery in the refusal of Congress to fulfill the terms concluded upon by their own general, disgraceful as they were to this country. But few of us know, that Mr. Laurens was the principal, if not the original adviser of this breach of faith of nations. He even added insult to injury; for instead of telling us openly, and with a manly confidence, that as the safety of the people was paramount to all conventions and stipulations between individuals, the troops could not be allowed to leave America, as this event would enable us to make such vigorous exertions as would probably destroy their beloved scheme of independence; he attempted to show, that what he had done was agreeable to the established notions of right, and this in a train of argument which its absurdity rendered unanswerable. It would have been as difficult to prove the truth of an axiom of Euclid, as to demonstrate the falsehood of the reasons, which Mr. Laurens published to the world in vindication of his conduct.

CORNWALLIS WRITES TO GERMAIN ABOUT VICTORY OVER
SOUTHERN ARMY
October 10, 1780

It is with great pleasure that I communicate to your Lordship an account of a complete victory obtained on the 16th instant by his Majesty's troops under my command, over the rebel Southern army commanded by General Gates.

CORNWALLIS REPORTS ON PRISONERS WITH PARDONS
October 11, 1780

An evening paper says, that Lord Cornwallis mentions in his private dispatches, that several of the prisoners taken in arms against the British forces had pardons in their pockets, signed by the commander in chief, exonerating them from any punishment for their past offenses, on condition of their taking the oath of allegiance to their lawful sovereign, the King of Great Britain. So little effect had this mark of clemency upon them that they had embraced the first opportunity to join General Gates, who received them with open arms, and advised them to carry their pardons in their pockets to the field; assuring them that Lord Cornwallis would not dare to injure them, but in all probability would restore them to their former situation. His Lordship, however, having too sensibly experienced the bad effects of temporizing, ordered several of them to be hanged up at headquarters.

COMMITMENT OF LAURENS TO TOWER OF LONDON
October 11, 1780

The commitment of Mr. Laurens to the Tower of London, by the three Secretaries of State on Friday last, runs thus:
These are in his Majesty's name, to authorize you to receive into your custody, the person of Henry Laurens, Esq., sent herewith on suspicion of high treason, whom you are to keep safe until he shall be delivered by due course of law: For so doing this is your warrant.
Stormont
Hilsborough
G. Germain

COUNT DE ROCHAMBEAU WRITES TO REPRESENTATIVES OF RHODE
ISLAND ASSEMBLY UPON HIS ARRIVAL THERE
October 18, 1780

Gentlemen,
The King, my master has sent me to the assistance of his good and
faithful allies, the United States of America. At present I only bring over
the vanguard of a much greater force, destined for their aid, and the King
has ordered me to assure them, that his whole power shall be exerted for
their support.

The French troops are under the strictest discipline and acting
under the orders of General Washington, will live with the Americans as
their brethren; and nothing will afford me greater happiness than con-
tributing to their success.

I am highly sensible of the marks of respect shown me by the General Assembly, and beg leave to assure them that as brethren, not only my
life, but the lives of the troops under my command are entirely devoted to
their service.

The Count De Rochambeau

A STATEMENT OF CORNWALLIS RE: AMERICANS
October 18, 1780

Articles of Intelligence from other daily papers.
The brave Lord Cornwallis seemed to have considered the number of
the Americans in the same light as Gam the Welch, captain in the reign
of Henry V did the numbers of the French; that there were enough to be
killed, enough to be taken prisoners, and enough to run away.

FRENCH PROCLAMATION IN AMERICA
October 21, 1780

The following translation of a proclamation published in America by
order of the French king, clearly points out to all the world the mischievous system of France.

PROCLAMATION
The persuasive love which has always animated the heart of the King
for the inhabitants of Canada, and the desire of withdrawing them from
the dominion of the English, have determined his Majesty to send into
one of the American ports land and sea forces, capable of effecting this
grand object. The moment of their arrival at the spot where they should
join the troops of the United States, the General of the two allied nations
will take care to concert the most speedy measures to fulfill the views of
Congress and the King in effecting the independence of Canada; and if
the French sly with joy to succour their distressed brethren, doubt not
they will hasten to shake off the yoke of the common enemy. The time is
at last arrived when Canada will be set free and in joining itself to the
thirteen independent states will bind again the cord of that strict friendship which unites them for ever to France...

Though very far from thinking that any French in Canada are capable of joining to spill the blood of his own brethren, this wisdom of his Majesty and the Congress engages them to forewarn the Canadians that the least succour given to British troops in their preparation of defense, in augmenting the difficulties and danger of the allies, should be considered by them as an act of hostility.

Monsieur the Count de Rochambeau, Lt. General of the King's army,....and Commander of his Majesty's army, will publish, after his arrival, a more particular invitation to join Canada to the confederacy of the United States; and we shall be charged to renew with the Canadians the fraternal disposition of said states, in the assembly to be called for that purpose. The instructions at present made public, communicate to the Canadians the design of his Majesty and the Congress of the United States for their deliverance, and to invite them to second our efforts in breaking themselves, the setters under which they groan.

> Lafayette
> by the General's order
> Capitaire, Secretary

WHO IS TO BLAME FOR BRITAIN'S NIGHTMARE?
October 30, 1780

To the Printer of *The Morning Chronicle*.

When the British nation is engaged in restoring a due subordination and obedience from its revolted Colonies, and at the same time involved in a combined war with France and Spain, unjustly entered into by them, for the express purpose of supporting that revolution, it becomes the duty of every Briton, animated with the least spark of national glory, or regard for the interest, prosperity, and happiness of himself and of his posterity, to exert every faculty to counteract and defeat their purpose. No person, the least conversant in the history of Europe can give the least faith to the declaration of France, that "as the Congress in America have declared themselves a free and independent people, they of right ought to be so;" and in support of such right, she has unsheathed the sword: If it was a real love of liberty, why does not that "friend to the rights of mankind" restore to seventeen millions of her own subjects that liberty she is so fond at the risk of a hazardous and expensive war, of securing to not more than three millions of the subjects of a neighbouring empire, distant three thousand miles from her? Will they not justly conclude it is done, not only with the express purpose of depressing this nation, by taking off such a number of its subjects, and depriving it of one of its greatest source of trade, but also to lesson its power and influence in Europe, which hitherto has set bounds, to the ambition of the House of Bourbon? Is it true the Spaniard, more politic than his Brother King, would not assign the same cause for his unjustly engaging in the war, as it affords so powerful a precedent for all Colonists to follow the example, and his interest might be too much affected by the same cause; but whatever his ostensible reasons may be, the real one is, to destroy the power and influence of Britain! Should this be true, as I believe no person will undertake to deny, is it not the interest of Europe in general to frustrate their pernicious schemes? Is it not in particular the duty of every Briton, to afford every support to his country in so trying a moment? On the event of which will depend, whether we shall continue to be a free and independent nation, or not. Now is the time for the great council of the nation to unite in every measure that may defeat the machinations of the common enemy, give support and vigour to the efforts necessary for our defense and preservation...

The Lords of the Admiralty have been condemned for being lulled by the intrigue and friendly assurances of France, at a time when they should have put our navy on the most respectable footing, so as to give them a great superiority over us at sea; should that be true, will complaints now remedy the evil? Unsuspicious is our national character, and they acted conformably to it; but have they not great merit in their exertions since, in establishing a naval force superior to France and Spain, in every quarter of the world, - why then, at this time, this complaint? The Cabinet have been blamed for starving the American war, when whoever will inspect the official letters, from and to, the Commander in Chief in that quarter, will find every requisition for troop and vessels of war has been fully complied with...

There must be some capital error somewhere; the nation has a right to enquire into the source of that error, that proper remedies may be applied. If Administration have been guilty of neglecting to send a force sufficient for the purpose of reducing the Colonists, in a fair and candid manner' point out their misconduct, that the public may be acquainted with it. If they, in this instance, have done their duty, let the true authors of the mischief be discovered, and held out to the indignation of their injured and abused country! If a Commander in Chief has frequently exposed his troops to the chances and carnage of a general engagement, and in the moment of victory has restrained their ardour, and ordered them to halt on the field of battle, without ever suffering the fugitives to be pursued? If the Commander in Chief has neglected any opportunity of capturing the whole American army, when he had it in his power to do it? If by neglecting to pursue the routed enemy after a defeat, the Commander has suffered the Americans to fortify themselves again within a few miles, so as to render the victory not only useless, but reduce him again to risque his troops to the carnage of other general engagement? I say, if these, or any of them have been done, or even any other duty neglected, sound policy, and the safety of the nation, require that a strict enquiry should be made into such misconduct...

I am an Englishman, but enlisted under no party: my sincere wish is, and it shall be the business of my life, to promote unanimity among my fellow citizens, to encourage every one to an exertion of those abilities with which Heaven has favoured us, to point out the causes of our present misfortunes, that we may avoid them in future; and have only to add, that these lines are written by a person unpensioned and unknown, either to one party or the other; one that is no man's enemy, and who would not for the universe rob any man of his good name; but at the same time, would use every endeavour to promote harmony and unanimity in the nation, and bring to light the authors of our present calamity, - which is all that is wanting to render us as powerful, as respectable, and happy as ever!

CHAPTER IV

November - December 1780

From
The Morning Chronicle and London Advertiser
(unless otherwise noted)

(All quotations, except headings)

THE HOUSE DEBATES WHETHER TO CONTINUE THE WAR (AFTER THE KING'S SPEECH TO PROSECUTE THE WAR WITH VIGOR)
November 9, 1780

HOUSE OF COMMONS

Mr. GRENVILLE...acknowledged that at the commencement of the war, Ministry had some pretext for pursuing the coercive measures which they adopted. At that time, it was said, and he believed it was truly said, that the voice of the nation was for war, the high spirit of this country being unwilling to give up our foreign and most valuable dependencies without a struggle. A struggle had been made, a vigorous struggle for many years; a struggle which this nation would feel for many, many years to come. At this time, he presumed, the voice of the nation was not for war, but for peace; peace at least, with America, if we should have war with the whole world besides. He could not, for these reasons, subscribe to an Address, which re-echoed a speech, professing an intention of prosecuting the American war with vigour; unless indeed, some one of the King's servants would rise and give the House reasons to expect better success than had yet blessed the British arms. If the Ministers had it in their power to prove to the satisfaction of the House, that it was wise to pursue the war with America, and that they had substantial grounds of assurance that it would shortly terminate honourably and happily for this country, let them do so, and he would agree to the King's Address as it stood; if they could not, he, for one, begged leave to utter his protest against the American war.

Mr. FITZPATRICK rose...and represented the impolicy of the present war with America, and recommended the withdrawing of our troops from thence, and concentring our force and directing it against the House of Bourbon; he adverted to the enormous increase of the national debt, the decay of manufactures and trade, the oppression of the people by taxes, etc, etc.

Sir Horace MANN thought that declamations tending to give the world an idea that our resources were exhausted, and that we ourselves were in a state of despondency, ill became Englishmen at any time, but least of all, in a moment of real difficulty and danger, in a moment when the most powerful confederacy that ever was formed, threatened us with destruction. It had been the character of this country to look danger in the face, to hold despair in contempt, and in proportion to the pressure of affairs, to exert its efforts, to act with spirit, and by the energy of its operations to surmount all difficulty and all resistance. This had been the practice of our ancestors, this ought to be the practice of Great Britain under her present circumstances. The American war was not ascribable to Administration, the seeds of it were deposited at a remoter period, but it was idle and absurd to be now losing time in accusations, and in fruitless attempts to charge any particular set of men as authors of the present difficulties; America had hostilely allied herself to France, the actual foe of Great Britain, and Spain had joined the confederacy. Each of the three powers who formed the league, were to be regarded with equal jealousy and to be opposed with equal exertion; America as well as France and Spain, France and Spain, as well as America. The interests of France and America were inseparably united...America, a Protestant people, declaring that she fought for her liberty, allied to France, a Roman Catholic power, in whose dictionary the word "liberty" had no place! Could any man in his senses for a moment believe that France had engaged in this expensive war, for the purpose of defending the liberties of America? The idea was too monstrous, and too ridiculous to be entertained for a moment. Was it likely that Spain, however drawn into the war by the intrigue of France, could be sincere in wishing to give America independency? Was it probable that she should have so little regard for her own interest, as to show herself a supporter of rebellion, and thus by her own example encourage all her South American Colonies to shake off their dependence on the Spanish Crown?...Looking at the confederacy in its proper light, seeing it in its true colours, was there not more cause to expect that so motley, so incongruous, so heterogeneous a mixture, so unnatural a League would not hold long together? France had already pretty plainly shown what were her views respecting America. America was already jealous of her, and every day that the war continued, she would have more and more cause to lament that she had ever called upon France to assist her...

Sir HORACE said...the American war began to wear a more promising aspect than it hitherto had done, and the prosecuting of it with vigour, was now more than ever, in his opinion, a necessary and wise measure. Our late successes were truly glorious, and the conduct of our officers, particularly that of Lord Cornwallis, merited the highest praise....He concluded with observing, that to renounce the American war would in his mind, be an act of political folly little short of madness; it would, at the same time, be an act of the greatest inhumanity, considering the number of loyalists, who had flocked in to the King's standard and who now relied on the British arms for protection.

Mr. TOWNSEND spoke...Every year, he said, Ministers gave a new reason to continue the American war; first, we were to send orders to deliver the men of consequence and property from the tyranny of the mob; afterwards to deliver the lower ranks from the oppression of the upper, and of the Congress; now we were called upon to deliver both from the captivity in which they were held by the French army. He lamented that if we were to continue the American war, which he looked upon as the favourite object of the Government, to that service all others were sacrificed. Ministers had sent young regiments under unexperienced officers to the West Indies, while our veterans were employed in North America.

Mr. Welbore ELLIS spoke...Would Gentlemen say, it was right for that House to hold a sullen silence on our late successes in America? Would it be handsome to Lord Cornwallis, or to the other officers who under the gallant Commander's orders, had acquitted themselves, so much to the credit of themselves and to the essential services of their country, to withhold their due praise? Or did Gentlemen imagine, if the eyes of all Europe were turned on the proceedings of that House (as had been truly observed) that it would have a good effect upon the minds of the foreign Princes and powers, to see the British Parliament, just at that moment, wanting in protections of zeal to his Majesty, or of joy at the late signal success of his Majesty's arms in America!...Another matter which struck him very forcibly, seemed to have made little or no impression on the Gentlemen, and that was, that as the King's Address containing due praises to the officers in America had been moved and seconded, the rejection of such an address would "ipso facto" amount to a censure upon those Officers and would have that effect in the eyes of all Europe. Would Gentlemen then say, they were prepared to pass a censure on the conduct of Lord Cornwallis and Colonel Tarleton? Would they even refuse to thank them for that conduct?

General SMITH spoke warmly against the King's Address. He contended that the American war was ruinous to this country...The General asserted, that we were in circumstances infinitely worse at present than at that unfortunate period of the Convention of Saratoga. The millions we had since spent upon the war would, he was well assured, have built and equipped fourty sail of the line. He declared that every military man knew, from the affair at Trenton, that all attempts to subdue America were so many fruitless prostitutions of blood and treasure, for that the matter was altogether impracticable. He therefore wished the House to tell his Majesty, they would go on with the American war no further, but would give every possible support to his arms, when directed against their proper object, - the House of Bourbon.

Mr. FOX rose...and said...At the present moment of embarrassment and distress, when the brightest jewel was torn from his diadem, when America was dissevered from the British empire, never to be reunited, when discord and civil desertions raged among those parts of the empire, which yet remained, but which seem prepared to revolt; to approach the throne with congratulatory addresses, was not loyalty, but cruel mockery and insult....How long, replied Mr. Fox, shall the sacred shield of majesty be interposed for the protection of a weak administration? This word majesty was a kind of hocus pocus word, which it turned into all shapes, and made subservient to every legerdemain trick, and every illusion convenience dictates. If by the blessing of his Majesty's government be understood his Majesty's personal virtues with respect and with reverence. But if by blessings of his government be understood the acts and projects of his Majesty's Ministers, he detested and reprobated them. The present reign had been one continuous series of disgrace, misfortune and calamity. What blessings are we called upon to recognize in the Address? First, the happy effect on this new Parliament, is giving his Majesty an opportunity of knowing the sentiments of his people. As an honourable friend of his had asked, was there no trick, no deceit used in orders to garble a new parliament? In words Ministers disclaimed the abridgement of the duration of septennial parliaments; in actions they approved it. He did not expect ever to see a septennial parliament die a natural death. Six years ago he observed, he had the honour to sit in the House, when the subject of their debate was precisely the same that it was this night, viz. the justice and expediency of prosecuting the American war; and he had no doubt, but that if he should have the honour to sit in the next parliament six year hence, at the opening of it, the same subject would be under discussion. It would have been presumption in him to have made such a prediction six years ago, and nobody would have credited him. Past experience now made it no longer so, and therefore he scrupled not to prophecy that if the war was continued, its propriety and its expediency would be the subject of discussion on the first opening of the next parliament. What have we gained by the American war in that period? We have exchanged Boston for New York; and Philadelphia, for Charlestown, O! but we have gained of late a most signal victory at Camden. General Gates and Sumpter are routed by Lord Cornwallis and Colonel Tarleton. These victories are but omens and forerunners of greater ones. Such was our sanguine expectation, when in the beginning of the war the British troops defeated the Americans on Long Island. The success at Brandywine was to be followed by the immediate reduction of the provinces and not a rebel was to be seen in all the Continent of North America.

The taking of Ticonderoga was a splendid affair; and that too was to be followed by the much important consequences. The event perpetually belied our sanguine predictions; yet now, with all our experience, we talk of following up with alacrity, our late victory in Carolina. That victory was a glorious one, he readily allowed, to the general officer, and all the officers and British troops who gained it; but the glory of that victory was due to the army only, and the disgrace of reducing Lord Cornwallis to that dangerous situation which made his victory a miracle, was the Minister's. The only fruit of the reduction of Charlestown was the dangerous situation that led necessarily to the engagement. The success of that engagement was alarming to him in another point of view. It was a proof that the majority of the Americans were not, as had been said, friendly to this country; but on the contrary, that they were almost unanimously attached to the cause of Congress. For no sooner did General Gates appear among the Carolinians, than those very men flocked to his standard, who had taken the oaths to our government, carrying along with them the arms that had been put into their hands by our General. This reduced Lord Cornwallis to the cruel necessity of putting them to death, and rendered that a necessary measure, which all who knew Lord Cornwallis, knew it must have given him infinite pain. Hence he argued, every gleam of success had been the certain forerunner of misfortune. The loss of the whole army followed the capture of Ticonderoga, the evacuation of Philadelphia had followed an other success; and no sooner do we hear of the surrender of Charlestown to his Majesty's arms, than we prepare to receive intelligence of some new disaster; and a very short time afterwards, news arrives of the loss of Rhode Island, which he was warranted to say, was the only good Winter harbour in all America.

Not that he meant to contend, that no advantage was to be derived from the late success obtained by the wonderful good conduct and gallantry of Lord Cornwallis. Great advantages might be derived from it, it might be made the foundation of an honourable and happy peace. Let Ministers seize and improve the advantage, and they will deserve the thanks and applause of their country...The war was begun madly, the Ministers made war blindfold, and the efforts of this country, so directed and so planned, like the efforts of a madman, which always were more powerful than those of a reasonable being, had astonished all Europe - but what good had they done? They had only weakened and reduced our resources. They had exhausted the spirits of the people and almost annihilated the power of future exertion...

But without ascribing to the Americans any extraordinary degrees of gratitude or perfidy, and considering them merely as men, whose conduct would, like that of other mortals, naturally be governed by a mixture of both reasons and passion, he thought they might be detached from the cause of the House of Bourbon, by omitting to pursue offensive hostilities against them.

What would be the consequence of withdrawing the troops from America? American independence undoubtedly. This would by the means of obtaining peace. If the American war could be given up without her being independent - let Ministers do it, but they could not. They were therefore wasting the blood and treasure of this country, without an object.

He said...We might carry on the war with greater success, by calling all our forces from America, and pouring them into the French settlements. As it was said in the last war that France was conquered in Germany, so if ever America was to be conquered, it must be in France...He was for beating France, rather than for railing at her, and he thought the best way to do that effectually, would be to pursue the war with America no longer; he was for turning the arms of this country solely against the House of Bourbon....

As to the particular commendations on a long list of Officers...Earl Cornwallis, who, he was ready to own, deserved the highest applause; but a right Honourable Gentleman had asked, would Gentlemen refuse to thank Lord Cornwallis, and his gallant officers, for their extraordinary gallantry at Camden? In answer to that question, he, for one made no scruple to declare, that he most certainly would; he would not thank his own brother, who was now serving in America, for any success he might obtain; as long as he lived, he never would agree to join in a vote of thanks to any officer, whose laurels were gathered in the American war; and his reason was, he hated and detested that war, he regarded it as the fountain head of all the mischief, and all the calamities, which this miserable country laboured under at this moment.

29

THE HOUSE CONTINUES THE DEBATE ON WAR AND THE AWARDS
TO BE GIVEN TO CLINTON AND CORNWALLIS
November 28, 1780

Mr. D. P. COKE, after a few introductory words said...As the House
had already heard from him, that he meant to move that their thanks be
voted to Lord Cornwallis, he thought it necessary that his present motion
went further, and took in another Officer, whose conduct was intimately
connected with the conduct of Lord Cornwallis...he could allude only to
Sir Henry Clinton.

With regard to the American war,....he declared, that as far as his
sentiments went, he was so fully convinced of the impolicy and danger of
this country's giving up all pretensions to sovereignty over America, that
the moment her independence was acceded to by Great Britain, he
should conceive the death warrant of the latter was signed. To prevent
so fatal a calamity, he declared, he would scruple not to vote away his
last shilling, and the last shilling of his constituents; With Ministers he
perfectly agreed as to the necessity of pursuing the recovery of the Sovereignty of Great Britain over America; it was with regard to the means
used by them for the attainment of that object, that he and most Gentlemen, he believed, differed from them. Their conduct wanted exertion
and it wanted firmness. When they were in the right, they ought to be
firm. To be otherwise, was a mark of impotency, dangerous to the State,
disgraceful to themselves. At present, they were in the right, and at
present it behooved them to show firmness.

Mr. COKE concluded with reading a motion: That the thanks of the
House be given to the Right Honourable Sir Henry Clinton, Knight of the
most honourable Order of the Bath, and Commander in Chief of his
Majesty's forces in America, and to the Right Honourable Charles Earl
Cornwallis, Lieutenant General of his Majesty's forces, for their great and
important services to this country, by the late signal victories obtained
over the Rebels in North America. Particularly to Sir Henry Clinton, for
his brave and wise conduct in the reduction of Charlestown, and to
Charles Earl Cornwallis, for his intrepidity and judgment in the glorious
action at Camden.

As soon as this motion was read, Lord NUGENT and Lord LEWI-
SHAM both rose to second it.

Alderman WILKES rose and said, he wished the Honourable Gentleman, who made the motion, would consent to withdraw it, because, let
him alter and amend it ever so much, he feared he would not be able to
render it acceptable to that side of the House, and for this reason:
because its object was to vote the thanks of the House to General Clinton
and Lord Cornwallis for having exerted themselves in a bad and wicked
cause. The American war, the Alderman said, was a wicked and unjust
war, began upon principles subversive of liberty, and which aimed directly at the destruction of the freedom of subject; for this reason, he never
would give his vote for any such motion; and let our success in America
be what it would, he should consider the inhabitants as having taken up
arms on the same principle that stimulated the people of England to take
up arms against Charles the First. That prince endeavoured to take

money out of the pockets of his subjects without their consent, the attempt was unconstitutional, and the people were warranted in taking up arms in defense of their undoubted rights. So the Americans were driven to the necessity of resistance, by this country's having unjustly endeavoured to take their money from them without their consent; he considered Sir Henry Clinton, and Lord Cornwallis, as having drawn their swords against their innocent fellow subjects, and as having unprovokedly bathed them in their blood. He was at the same time as ready to allow, that Lord Cornwallis had behaved with great gallantry at Camden, as any Honourable Gentleman present, but what was he to think of an Officer, who had possessed the same opinion of the American war which he did, and nevertheless had himself carried fire and sword against the Americans. Lord Cornwallis had told him some years ago, that he disapproved of the American War, and that he did not think this country had any right to exercise taxation over America. This sentiment that noble Earl had expressly subscribed to by a formal protest upon the subject in the year 1773, which he signed with four other Peers. The Alderman, said he would readily agree to join in a vote of thanks to any officer who obtained a victory over our natural foes, France and Spain.

Lord NORTH expressed his concern...that the Honourable Gentleman who spoke last had endeavoured to cast an imputation upon Lord Cornwallis, which that noble and gallant officer by no means deserved...The Hon. Gentleman had charged Lord Cornwallis with having drawn his sword in America in contradiction to his own sentiments. He denied the assertion, and he would venture to say, it was not in the Hon. Gentleman's power to prove his words...Lord Cornwallis was no soldier of fortune; his high rank, his ample estate, his distinguished connections, his near relationship to those who filled the first offices in church and state, rendered his own country not only dear to him, but pregnant with everything which his utmost wishes could expect. What then could induce Lord Cornwallis to quit a country, where he was so situated, but that nice feeling, which belonged to every brave and worthy officer, a desire to serve well of his country, a desire to promote her dearest interests? These and these only were the motives that Lord Cornwallis had been actuated by, and he believed the Honourable Gentleman who spoke last was the only man in that House, who wished to sully the fair fame of so exalted a character as that of Lord Cornwallis, or who was ready to question the purity of the impulse, influenced by which, Lord Cornwallis was now cheerfully undergoing all the toils of the American service. With regard to the protest which the Hon. Gentleman had alluded to, he remembered, it was a protest against the Declaratory Law, containing grounds of argument similar to those urged by a member of that House, now no more, and supported by just about as large a number of Gentlemen as there had been Peers names subscribed.

Mr. WILKES rose to explain, and at the same time to complain of the noble Lord's having misrepresented him. He had never said Lord Cornwallis was a soldier of fortune or anything like it; he had declared that Lord Cornwallis had subscribed a protest in concert with four other Peers, stating among other arguments, that this country had no right to exercise the power of taxation over America.

Sir Charles BUNBURY said, he had expected a motion merely to thank Lord Cornwallis, and to such a motion he was ready to have given his consent, had it been properly worded; that extending the motion to one other name might give room for gentlemen all around the House to move amendments, in order to have the name of some military or naval friend or other enrolled....The singular bravery and the extra-ordinary good conduct of Lord Cornwallis in the affair of Camden, were matters which had excited the admiration and wonder, not only of common observers, but of the whole military profession; that then he considered as a fit cause for voting the thanks of the Thanks of the House to Lord Cornwallis. The reduction of Charlestown certainly was an essential piece of service, but though he was far from denying that the gallant conduct of Sir Henry Clinton had great merit, he could not regard it in any other light than as a common transaction of the war. If it were considered in any other light, ought not the eminent services of other officers to be remembered at the same time? Why should not General Prevail's name be inserted in the Motion? He was surely entitled to the Thanks of the House, for having defended Savannah against the efforts of Monsieur D'Estaing, at the head of a French army, aided by an army of Americans.

With regard to the present Motion, Sir Charles did not approve of the wording of it. He thought the sole business of any motion of that sort, was to state the fact for which the Thanks of the House were voted, without comment or argument. The present motion not only stated the facts pretty amply, but contained an argument, which bound down every Gentleman, who voted for it, to an opinion in favour of the American War. Why insert the words "great and important services?" What was that but a comment consequent to the motion itself? Did it not imply, that every Gentleman, who voted for the Motion approved of the American War, and thought that every victory gained in the progress of that most unfortunate and calamitous business, was "a great and important service?" This was a doctrine, which he for one, was by no means ready to adopt; he hoped therefore, if unanimity was wished for, that the motion should be still further amended, and those words, which he had objected to, omitted.

Sir Joseph MOWBRY strongly objected to the whole motion and urged a great number of arguments to prove that no gentleman who disapproved of the American war, could with the least consistency agree to it.

The whole amended motion was ultimately put, and carried without a division.

EXCERPTS OF PROCLAMATION BY GENERAL ARNOLD
December 1, 1780

From Rivington's *New York Gazette*, November 1.

To the Officers and Soldiers of the Continental Army, who have the Real Interest of their Country at heart, and who are determined to be no longer the tools and dupes of Congress, or of France.

Friends, fellow soldiers and citizens, arise and judge for yourselves, - reflect on what you have lost, - consider to what you are reduced, and by your courage repel the ruin that will threaten you.

Your country once was happy and had the proffered peace been embraced, your last two years of misery would have been spent in peace and plenty, and repairing the desolations of quarrel that would have set the interest of Great Britain and America in its true light and cemented their friendship; whereas you are now the prey of avarice, the scorn of your enemies and the pity of your friends.

You were promised Liberty by the leaders of your affairs; but is there an individual in the enjoyment of it, saving your oppressors? Who among you dare speak, or write what he thinks, against the tyranny which has robbed you of your property, imprisons your persons, drags you to the field of battle, and is daily deluging your country with your blood?

You are flattered with Independency as preferably to a redress of grievances, and for that shadow, instead of real felicity, are sunk into all the wretchedness of poverty by the rapacity of your own rulers. Already are you disqualified to support the pride of character, they taught you to aim at, and must inevitably shortly belong to one or other of the great powers, their folly and wickedness have drawn into conflict. Happy for you, that you may still become the fellow subjects of Great Britain, if you nobly disdain to be vassals of France.

What is America now but a land of widows, orphans and beggars? - and should the parent nation cease her exertions to deliver you, what security remains to you even for the enjoyment of the consolations of that religion for which your fathers braved the ocean, the heathen, and the wilderness? Do you know that the eye which guides this pen, lately saw your mean and prostigate Congress at Mass, for the soul of a Roman Catholic in Purgatory, and participating in the rites of the Church, against whose anti-christian corruptions, your pious ancestors would have witnessed with their blood?

As to you, who have been soldiers in the continental army, can you at this day want evidence that the funds of your country are exhausted, or that the managers have applied them to their own private uses? In either case you surely can no longer continue in their service with honour or advantage; yet you have hitherto been their supporters in that cruelty, which, with an equal indifference to yours, as well as to the labour and blood of others, is devouring a country, that from the moment you quit their colours, will be redeemed from their tyranny.

But what need of arguments to such, as feel infinitely more misery than tongue can express. I therefore only add my promise of the most affectionate welcome and attention, to all who are disposed to join me in the measures necessary to close the scene of our afflictions, which intolerable as they are, must continue to increase until we have the wisdom (shown of late by Ireland) in being contended with the liberality of the Parent Country, who still offers her protection, with the immediate restoration of our ancient privileges, civil and sacred, and a perpetual exemption from all taxes, but such as shall think fit to impose on ourselves.

B. Arnold

ANOTHER MOTION IS MADE OF "THANKS OF THE HOUSE"
December 12, 1780

A Motion was made by Daniel Parker COKE, Esq., Member for Nottingham, seconded by Lord LEWISHAM, Member for the County of Stafford, and after various Amendments put by the Speaker in the following words: That the Thanks of this House be given to Sir Henry Clinton, Knight of the Most Honourable Order of the Bath, and Commander in Chief of his Majesty's Forces in North America; and to Vice Admiral Arbuthnot, Commander in Chief of his Majesty's Fleet in North America; and to the Right Honourable Lieutenant General Charles Earl Cornwallis; for the eminent and very important Services performed by them to his Majesty and this country, particularly by the reduction of Charlestown by the Army and Navy under the Command of Sir Henry Clinton and Vice-Admiral Arbuthnot, and by the late most glorious victory obtained by Lord Cornwallis at Camden.

CORNWALLIS ANNOUNCES SUCCESS IN DEFEATING GENERAL SUMPTER'S CORPS
December 18, 1780

From *The South Carolina Gazette*, September 14.
Lord Cornwallis's Orders:
Lord Cornwallis is happy to announce to this army, the great success of Lieut. Col. Tarleton, who with a detachment of light infantry, cavalry and infantry of the legion, consisting of two hundred and fifty, came up with and defeated Brigadier General Sumpter's corps...
Lord Cornwallis returns his warmest thanks to the officers and soldiers of the light infantry and legion for their great services and distinguished bravery and he assures Lieut. Col. Tarleton, that his great and eminent services shall never be forgotten by him, and that he will endeavour to do him justice in the accounts which he shall transmit to his Sovereign.

DISPATCHES ON THE WAR AT SEA
December 18, 1780

The French and Spaniards have contrived, by sending their fleet to sea at this time and not before, to gain a superiority over us, which without any brilliant conquest will bring decisive advantage to their campaign. They have obliged us to keep our grand force at sea, tearing them to pieces without action, while the greater part of theirs was laid safe in port, undamaged and unweakened by cruising. Previous to this time they knew that we could not attempt to throw reinforcements into Gibraltar. Our trade must be protected out and in. The time has now come, however, when that important garrison must be relieved. They stand in need of fresh provisions, and of all kinds of military stores. But the enemy have come to sea and at a season when they used to be driven, beaten and disabled, into their ports, and when the sea and all that was therein, was left to Britain, and seeking whom they may devour. We cannot now relieve Gibraltar, and that great and useful possession will be brought into distress, which must alarm us for its safety. This is the situation of our affairs, and yet we have been proudly told of the glory of the present campaign. It is more than probable, that the loss of Gibraltar will be added to the success which has this year crowned our arms.

EXTRACT OF A LETTER FROM DUBLIN
December 20, 1780

It was yesterday very currently reported in town, that five out the twelve United States of America had sent delegates to Gen. Clinton with proposals of an amnesty to be under the protection of Great Britain.

Great jealousies subsist at present among the officers of the American army at Rhode Island, on account of the French officers getting a superiority of command.

The correspondent who sent us the above mentions, that Count Rochambeau was challenged by a Lieut. General of the Continental army, which he refused.

The privates in general of both armies look on each with a jealous eye. They cry in open camp, Peace with Great Britain, or an exclusion of Frenchmen.

A gentleman lately from New York says, so tired are the Americans of the present unhappy war, that the privates in the service of Congress affront their officers on parade, insomuch that a common sentinel, aided by several others, had, on the 13th of Sept. seized 14 officers and put them in close confinement.

LOYALISTS IN CHARLESTON THANKING CORNWALLIS
December 27, 1780

From *The South Carolina and American General Gazette* of October 14, 1780.

We his Majesty's dutiful and loyal subjects, inhabitants of Charlestown,...take this opportunity...of tendering to your Lordship, our joyful congratulation on the total defeat and dispersions of the rebel army by his Majesty's forces under your command.

When we reflect on the desolation and ruin with which this province was threatened, by the unrelenting cruelty of a formidable and menacing enemy, we think ourselves fortunate, that we had no idea of our danger, until we were effectually delivered from it by the glorious victory obtained by your Lordship,...which inspires us with gratitude to the supreme ruler of the universe; and, at the same time, excites in our minds, a due sense of the manifold obligations we have to your Lordship, for your distinguished conduct and courage, so eminently conspicuous in the accomplishment of that great event; which has rescued this province from impending destruction, and is no less advantageous to our most gracious Sovereign and the British Empire, than honourable to your Lordship...We cannot but consider the late attempt of Congress to subjugate the freemen of this province to their tyrannical domination, as an additional proof of their restless ambition, and of the wicked machinations of the contemptible remains of the expiring faction, who have so recently exercised a despotic and lawless sway over us; and, we trust, that every other hostile experiment, by the goodness of God, and your Lordship's vigilance and animated endeavours, will be rendered equally futile.

That Heaven, propitious to your Lordship's active zeal in the service of your King and country, may crown your future exertions with success, and incline our deluded Sister Colonies to partake of those blessings, of which we have so fair a prospect, are the sincere and ardent wishes not only of us, but we are persuaded, of every other loyal inhabitant of Charlestown.

September 19, 1780 (signed by about 100 people)

CORNWALLIS'S ANSWER TO THE LOYALISTS OF CHARLESTON
December 27, 1780

It gives me great pleasure to be assured by you, that my conduct has merited the approbation of the loyal inhabitants of Charlestown. I shall always endeavour, to the utmost of my abilities, to contribute to the honour and prosperity of my King and country, and to the release of his Majesty's loyal subjects in America, from the cruel and oppressive tyranny under which they have so long and so severely suffered.

Cornwallis

PROCLAMATION BY CORNWALLIS
December 27, 1780

Whereas the enemies of his Majesty's Government continuing to practice every artifice and deceit to impose on the minds of the people, have as industriously, as falsely, propagated a belief among the people of this country, that the King's army indiscriminately makes war, and commits ravages upon the placable inhabitants, and those who are in arms and open rebellion against his Majesty's authority; I think it proper, in order to remove such false and injurious impressions, and to restore as much peace and quiet to the country as may be possible, during the operations of war, hereby to assure the people at large, that all of those who come into the posts of his Majesty's army under my command, and faithfully deliver up their army and give a military parole to remain thenceforth peaceably at home, doing no offense against his Majesty's Government, will be protected in their persons and properties, and be paid a just and fair price in gold or silver, for whatever they may furnish for the use of the King's army; it being his Majesty's most gracious wish and intention, rather to reclaim his deluded subjects to a sense of their duty, and obedience to the laws, by justice and mercy, than by the force and terror of his arms.

27th of September   Cornwallis

THE GENERAL ARNOLD - MAJOR ANDRE AFFAIR
December 2, 1780

EXTRACTS OF WASHINGTON'S LETTERS TO CONGRESS

Robinson's House in the Highlands, September 26, 1780.

I have the honour to inform Congress, that I arrived here yesterday about twelve o'clock, on my return from Hartford. Some hours previous to my arrival, Major General Arnold went from his quarters, which were this place, and as it was supposed, over the river to the garrison at West Point, whither I proceeded myself, in order to visit the post. I found General Arnold had not been there during the day, and on my return to his quarters, he was still absent. In the mean time, a packet had arrived from Lieutenant Colonel Jamieson, announcing the capture of a John Anderson, who was endeavouring to go to New York with several interesting and important papers, all in the handwriting of General Arnold. This was also accompanied with a letter from the prisoner, avowing himself to be Major John Andre, Adjutant General to the British army, relating the manner of his capture and endeavouring to show, that he did not come under the description of a spy. From these several circumstances, and information, that the General seemed to be thrown into some degree of agitation on receiving a letter a little time before he went from his quarters, I was led to conclude immediately that he had heard of Major Andre's captivity, and that he would, if possible, escape to the enemy, and accordingly took such measures as appeared the most probable to apprehend him. But he had embarked in a barge and proceeded down the river, under a flag, to the Vulture ship of war, which lay at some miles below Stoney and Verplank's Point. He wrote me a letter after he got on board. Major Andre is not arrived yet, but I hope he is secure, and that he will be here today. I have been, and am taking precautions, which I trust will prove effectual to prevent the important consequences which this conduct, on the part of General Arnold, was intended to produce. I do not know the party that took Major Andre, but it is said, that it consisted only of a few militia, who acted in such a manner upon the occasion, as does them the highest honour, and proves them to be men of great virtue. As soon as I know their names, I shall take pleasure in transmitting them to Congress.

Paramus, October 7, 1780.

I have the honour to enclose to Congress a copy of the proceedings of a board of General Officers in the case of Major Andre, Adjutant General to the British army. This officer was executed in pursuance of the opinion of the board, on Monday the 2nd inst. at twelve o'clock, at our late camp at Tappan. Besides the proceedings I transmit copies of sundry letters respecting the matter, which are all that passed on the subject, not included in the proceeding...Proceedings of a Board of General Officers, held by order of his Excellency General Washington, Commander in Chief of the Army of the United States of America, respecting Major Andre, Adjutant General to the British Army, September the 29th, 1780, at Tappan, in the State of New York.

(15 generals were present)

Major Andre, Adjutant General to the British Army was brought before the Board, and the following letter from General Washington, to the Board, dated Head Quarters, Tappan, September 29, 1780, was laid before them and read:

Major Andre, Adjutant General to the British Army will be brought before you for your examination. He came within our lines in the night, on an interview with Major General Arnold, and in an assumed character, and was taken within our lines, in a disguised habit, with a pass under a feigned name, and with the enclosed papers concealed upon him. After a careful examination, you will be pleased, as speedily as possible, to report a precise state of his case, together with your opinion of the light in which he ought to be considered, and the punishment that ought to be inflicted. The Judge Advocate will attend to assist in the examination, who has sundry other papers relative to this matter, which he will lay before the Board.

G. Washington

THE BOARD OF GENERAL OFFICERS CONVENED AT TAPPAN

The names of the officers composing the Board were read to Major Andre...and asked whether he confessed the matters contained in the letter, from his Excellency General Washington to the Board, or denied them; he said, in addition to his letter to General Washington, dated Salem, the 24th of September 1780, (which was read to the Board, and acknowledged by Major Andre, to have been written by him), which letter is as follows:

Salem, 24th September 1780.

What I have as yet said concerning myself was in the justifiable attempt to be extricated; I am too little accustomed to duplicity to have succeeded.

I beg your Excellency will be persuaded, that no alteration in the temper of my mind, or apprehension for my safety, induces me to take the step of addressing you, but that is to secure myself from an imputation of having assumed a mean character for treacherous purposes or self-interest. A conduct incompatible with the principles that actuated me, as well as with my condition in life.

It is to vindicate my same that I speak and not to solicit security.

The person in your possession is Major John Andre, Adjutant General to the British army.

The influence of one commander in the army of his adversary, is an advantage taken in war. A correspondence for this purpose I held; as confidential (in the present instance) with his Excellency Sir Henry Clinton.

To savour it, I agreed to meet upon ground not within posts of either army, a person who was to give me intelligence; I came up in the Vulture man of war for this effect, and was fetched by a boat from the shore to the beach. Being there I was told, that the approach of day would prevent my return, and that I must be concealed until the next night. I was in my regimentals and had fairly risked my person.

38

Against my stipulation, my intention and without my knowledge before hand, I was conducted within one of your posts. Your Excellency may conceive my sensation on this occasion and will imagine how much more must I have been affected, by a refusal to reconduct me back the next night as I had been brought. Thus become a prisoner, I had to concert my escape. I quitted my uniform, and was passed another way in the night without the American posts to neutral ground, and informed I was beyond all armed parties and left to press for New York, I was taken to Tarry Town by some volunteers.

Thus, as I have had the honour to relate, was I betrayed (being Adjutant General of the British army) into the vile condition of an enemy in disguise within your posts.

Having avowed myself a British Officer, I have nothing to reveal but what relates to myself, which is true on the honour of an officer and a gentleman.

The request I have to make, your Excellency, and I am conscious I address myself well, is, that in any rigor policy may dictate, a decency of conduct towards me may mark, that though unfortunate, I am branded with nothing dishonourable as no motive could be mine but the service of my King, and as I was involuntarily an impostor.

Another request is, that I may be permitted to write an open letter to Sir Henry Clinton, and another to a friend for clothes and linen.

I take the liberty to mention the condition of some gentlemen at Charlestown, who being either on parole or under protection, were engaged in a conspiracy against us. Though their situation is not similar, they are subjects who may be set in exchange for me, or are persons whom the treatment I received might affect.

It is no less Sir, in a confidence in the generosity of your mind than on account of your superior station, that I have chosen to importune you with this letter

John Andre

The following papers were laid before the board and shown to Major Andre, who confessed to the board that they were found on him when he was taken, and said they were concealed in his boot, except the pass:--

A pass from General Arnold to John Anderson, which name Major Andre acknowledged be affirmed.

Artillery Order, September 5, 1780

Estimate of the force at West Point and its dependencies, September, 1780.

Return of Ordnance at West Point, September, 1780.

Remarks on works at West Point.

Copy of a State of Matters, laid before a Council of War, by his Excellency General Washington, held the 6th of September 1780.

A letter signed John Anderson, dated September 7, 1780, to Colonel Sheldon...

Major Andre having acknowledged the preceding facts, and being asked whether he had anything to say respecting them, answered that he left them to operate with the Board.

The examination of Major Andre being concluded, he was remanded into custody.

The following letters were laid before the board and read:

(1) Benedict Arnold's letter to General Washington, dated September 25, 1780.

On Board the Vulture.

The heart which is conscious of its own rectitude, cannot attempt to palliate a step which the world may censure as wrong; I have ever acted from a principle of love to my country, since the commencement of the present unhappy contest between Great Britain and the Colonies; the same principle of love to my country actuates my present conduct, however, it may appear inconsistent to the world, who very seldom judge right of any man's actions.

I have no favour to ask for myself. I have too often experienced the ingratitude of my country to attempt it; but from the known humanity of your Excellency, I am induced to ask your protection for Mrs. Arnold, from every insult and injury that a mistaken vengeance of my country may expose her to. It ought to fall only on me; she is as good and as innocent as an angel and is incapable of doing wrong; I beg she may be permitted to return to her friends in Philadelphia, or to come to me, as she may choose. From your Excellency I have no fears on her account, but she may suffer from the mistaken fury of the country.

I have to request that the enclosed letter may be delivered to Mrs. Arnold, and she permitted to write to me.

I have also to ask, that my clothes and baggage, which are of little consequence, may be sent to me; if required, their value shall be paid in money.

B. Arnold

N.B. In justice to the gentlemen of my family, Col. Varrick and Major Franks, I think myself in honour bound to declare, that they, as well as Joshua Smith, Esq. (who I know is suspected) are totally ignorant of any transaction of mine, that they had reason to believe were injurious to the public.

(2) Colonel Robinson's letter to General Washington, dated September 25, 1780.

Vulture, off Sinfink.

I am this moment informed, that Major Andre, Adjutant General of his Majesty's army in America, is detailed as a prisoner by the army under your command. It is therefore incumbent on me to inform you of the manner of his falling into your hands. He went up with a flag, at the request of General Arnold, on public business with him, and had his permit to return by land to New York, Under these circumstances Major Andre cannot be detained by you, without the greatest violation of flags, and contrary to the custom and usage of all nations; and as I imagine you will see this matter in the same point of view as I do, I must desire you will order him to be set at liberty, and allowed to return immediately. Every step Major Andre took, was by the advice and direction of General Arnold, even that of taking a feigned name, and of course not liable to censure for it.

Col. Robinson

(3) General Clinton's letter, dated the 26th of September, 1780.
New York.

Being informed that the King's Adjutant General in America has been stopped, under Major General Arnold's passports, and is detained a prisoner in your Excellency's army, I have the honour to inform you, Sir, that I permitted Major Andre to go to Major General Arnold, at the particular request of that General Officer. You will perceive, Sir, by the enclosed paper, that a flag of truce was sent to receive Major Andre, and passports granted for his return. I therefore can have no doubt but your Excellency will immediately direct, that this officer has permission to return to my orders at New York.

H. Clinton

(Enclosed letter of the 26th of Sept, 1780, from Benedict Arnold to General Clinton).

In answer to your Excellency's message respecting your Adjutant General, Major Andre, and desiring my idea of the reasons why he is detained, being under my passports, I have the honour to inform you, Sir, that I apprehend a few hours must return Major Andre to your Excellency's orders, as that officer is assuredly under the protection of a flag of truce, sent by me to him, for the purpose of a conversation, which I requested to hold with him relating to myself, and which I wished to communicate through that officer, to your Excellency.

I commanded, at the time, at West Point, had an undoubted right to send my flag of truce for Major Andre, who came to me under that protection, and having held my conversation with him, I delivered him confidential papers in my own handwriting, to deliver to your Excellency; thinking it much properer he should return by land, I directed him to make use of the feigned name of John Anderson, under which he had by my direction, come on shore and gave him my passports to go to the White Plains on his way to New York. This officer cannot therefore fail of being immediately sent to New York, as he was invited to a conversation with me, for which I sent him a flag of truce, and finally gave him passports for his safe return to your Excellency. All of which I had then a right to do, being in the actual service of America, under the orders of General Washington, and Commanding General at West Point, and its dependencies.

B. Arnold

The Board having considered the letter from his Excellency, General Washington, respecting Major Andre, Adjutant General to the British Army, the confession of Major Andre, and the papers produced to them, REPORT to his Excellency, the Commander in Chief, the following facts, which appear to them relative to Major Andre:

First, That he came on shore from the Vulture sloop of war, in the night of the 21st of September, inst. on an interview with General Arnold, in a private and secret manner.

Second, That he changed his dress, within our lines and under a feigned name, and in a dignified habit, passed our works at Stoney and Verplunk's Points, the evening of the 22nd of September inst. and was taken the morning of the 23rd of Sept. inst, at Tarry Town, in a disguised habit, being then on his way to New York, and when taken he had in his possession several papers, which contained intelligence for the enemy.

The Board having maturely considered these facts, do also report to his Excellency General Washington that Major Andre, Adjutant General to the British Army, ought to be considered as a spy from the enemy, and that agreeable to the law and usage of nations, it is their opinion - he ought to suffer death.

Copy of a Letter from Major Andre to Sir Henry Clinton.
Tappan, September 29, 1780.

Your Excellency is doubtless already apprised of the manner in which I was taken and possibly of the serious light in which my conduct is considered, and the rigorous determination that is impending.

Under these circumstances, I have obtained General Washington's permission to send you this letter; the object of which is, to remove from your breast any suspicion, that I could imagine I was bound by your Excellency's order, to expose myself to what has happened. The events of coming within an enemy's posts, and of changing my dress, which led me to my present situation, were contrary to my own intentions, as they were to your orders; and the cirepitous route, which I took to return, was imposed (perhaps unavoidably) without alternative upon me.

I am perfectly tranquil in mind, and prepared for any fate, to which an honest zeal for my King's service may have devoted me.

In addressing myself to your Excellency on this occasion, the force of all my obligations to you and of the attachment and gratitude I bear you, recurs to me. With all the warmth of my heart, I give you thanks for your Excellency's profuse kindness to me; and I send you the most earnest wishes for your welfare, which a faithful, affectionate, and respectful attendant can frame.

I have a mother and three sisters to whom the value of my commission would be an object, as the loss of Grenada has much affected their income. It is needless to be more explicit on this subject; I am persuaded of your Excellency's goodness.

I receive the greatest attention from his Excellency General Washington, and from every person under whose charge I happen to be placed.
                                                    John Andre

(After an exchange of a number of more letters from both the British and American side) the following was published by order of Congress):

The time which elapsed between the capture of Major Andre, which was the 23rd of September, and his execution, which did not take place till twelve o'clock on the 2nd of October, the mode of trying him, his letter to Sir Henry Clinton...in which he said "I receive the greatest attention from his Excellency General Washington and from every person under whose charge I happen to be placed;" not to mention many other acknowledgements which he made of the good treatment he received; must evince, that the proceedings against him were not guided by passion or resentment, The practice and usage of war were against his request, and made the indulgence he solicited, circumstanced as he was, inadmissible.

                                        Charles Thompson, Sec.

(The above account having been published by Congress it may, without any violent strain of probability, be conjectured that they thought General Washington's severity to Major Andre stood in need of some apology. How far the Congress account justifies General Washington's conduct towards the brave Andre, the public will judge for themselves.)

MAJOR ANDRE'S GHOST WRITES TO LORD NORTH
December 9, 1780

...Listen, oh listen to the voice of truth speaking from the grave. Your country sends forth her armies to crush what she pronounces to be rebellion. The first Minister of the State, upon a critical and signal occasion, obliquely contravenes the sentence of the laws, by resolving the guilt of rebellion for rebellion it is, most rank and foul, into the mere necessity of hostile opposition. This procedure will be the accession of ten thousand men, to the cause of rebellion. The speculation upon it in Europe and America will re-establish her funds, and give currency to her fictitious money, The hapless tribe of loyalists, who have so long been stretched on the faces of persecution, will suspect they have no other prospect before them, but of continuing in the same flat, exalted into keener anguish by the contemplation of their executioners stretched on beds of roses, But beware, for prudence, if not for pity, my Lord, of lacerating the hearts of men, and mated by the purest principles that ever adorned any cause, in any country. Presume not too far upon their virtue, their patience and their attachment, lest you torture them into despair; for out of despair, resentment, and revenge may grow direful reverse! Should their generous spirits enter into the mass of rebellion it will then indeed soon take another name, and Empire will have finished her journey to the West.

I must be brief. Mark this livid circle, which is still suffered to stain my neck, to alarm, to rouse you from that deep, that profound lethargy which has benighted your soul. Think not that I lament my fate, for know, that the vilest indignities which my mortal part could suffer from the hand of rebellion, are ennobled in my fall. But mark, oh mark this stain! and think what reparation you owe to that desolated house, whose prop, whose pride, whose darling I was, by standing forth the palliator of my murder; - but Angels summon me away - be warned!

EXPLANATION OF ARNOLD'S DEFECTION
December 27, 1780

It is said, that when General Arnold went into New York, he declared himself as much attached to America as ever, but being convinced from every circumstance, that either Great Britain or France must govern her (and that the latter, though the least improbable, was the choice of those in power, in hopes of retaining their importance), this consideration determined him to throw up his command and offer his service, in whatever station his Excellency General Sir Henry Clinton thought proper to employ him to assist in frustrating the intentions of France, and bringing back the Colonies to their allegiance to Great Britain.

CHAPTER V

January - December 1781

From
The Morning Chronicle and London Advertiser
(unless otherwise noted)

(All quotations, except headings)

INTERCEPTED REBEL MAIL, PRINTED FROM *THE NEW YORK ROYAL GAZETTE EXTRAORDINARY* (EXCERPTS)
January 27, 1781

Schuylkill Falls, November 15, 1780.
Some time has elapsed since I wrote you last owing to my having been ill with the fever which raged in the city....I was compelled to move to this place for recovery of health, from which I ride into the city every morning to meet Committees at nine, attend Congress afterwards, and return at night...I am sorry to say, that they are far from affording pleasure to the friends of America; former Congresses undoubtedly had their difficulties, and whether any other set of men under their circumstances would have done better, is not easy for a judicious mind to determine. Events have however proved their error, and call for a speedy reformation. Perhaps most of our difficulties have arisen from our ignorance of finance, and the want of system in every department.
A new army is now arranged, the States now called upon for men and specific supplies. All public departments are now arranging upon economical principles; the several and expensive navy boards will be abolished. The war-office and treasury board regulated. A Committee is appointed, for arranging our finances. A loan from France solicited in the most pressing and positive terms, and a regular system will soon take place. Perhaps it may be thought a late hour for this reformation, but is it not better late than never? Every day's experience proves, that many of our distresses arise from a want of power in Congress to carry any of their measures into execution. They send requisitions to the states, some comply, some do not, and the consequence of this is too obvious to need explanation; hence it is that our army is often ready to perish with hunger and cold...At present we have no money in the Treasury; some states have not yet received their new money, or called in their old. This, with the artful industry of Tories and speculators, has depreciated the old money to eighty-five, and even to an hundred and ten for

45

one in this city. This of course more than doubles our national debt...In short, this season has exhibited a scene of misfortunes, scarcely to be equalled in history, many of them have arisen from unforeseen events; and too many from our own inattention and neglect. Measures are now taken for forwarding the arms and clothing. But to prevent the other evils arising from depreciation and speculation is not so easy.

John Sullivan

THE DUTCH ENTER THE WAR!
(EXCERPTS OF HOUSE OF COMMONS DEBATE)
January 30, 1781

Lord LEWISHAM said it had been proved to the conviction of every man, that the Dutch had long been employed in assisting France with warlike stores, and it had for some time been suspected that they were inclined rather to give aid to the revolted Colonies of America, than to comply with the faith of treaties, and perform what Holland had solemnly pledged herself to perform, whenever her ancient Ally was attacked by the House of Bourbon, and made the requisitions prescribed by the Treaty of Westminster. Her failure to do Great Britain justice had been evident and her inclinations towards America were now equally evident; nothing, he conceived could have induced the States to act the part they had lately exhibited, but the baneful influence of French gold, which had so far prevailed as to make the Dutch deal thus treacherously by us; therefore he thought his Majesty entitled to the most cordial thanks of the House, and their most loyal professions of zeal and attachment, as well as an immediate assurance of their determination to support the vigorous measures his Majesty had resolved to pursue, since every man must agree that it was better to have an open enemy, than a treacherous friend.

Lord NORTH said that unfortunately the policy of Europe has changed of late years and Holland, though her ruin must inevitably follow the ruin of Great Britain, should the House of Bourbon succeed, rejects the old policy and adopts the new one; she is no longer the friend and ally of Great Britain, but has joined France, and broke her faith with this country through the influence and under the direction of France. Great Britain has uniformly adhered to her old system and inviolably complied with the express conditions of her treaties, whenever her allies were attacked, and claimed her assistance. Unfortunately for Great Britain, the other powers of Europe have not acted with equal fidelity.

WHO COULD OR WOULD BE ENGLAND'S ALLY?
(HOUSE OF COMMONS DEBATE - CONT.)
January 31, 1781

Mr. WRAXALL spoke...In this crisis where were we to find protection? How retrieve our former situation?...Wraxall demonstrated the necessity of our procuring an immediate ally on the continent; a doctrine which he enforced with the strongest arguments, and with all the zeal and ardour of a man speaking from the impulse of the fullest conviction. He ended this head of his speech with asking, Who was to be this Ally?

And in order to prepare the House for the mention of the power whose alliance he thought most likely to be of service to us, he drew a picture of Europe as it stood at the present time.

He first began with a description of Denmark, which he spoke of as a nation of pirates...He next called the attention of the House to Sweden, governed by a King rendered absolute by French money in 1772. Swedes, he said, ever since Christina, had been uniformly the Ally of France...

He then took a view of Russia and described the Empress and her character on which he passed a warm eulogium. He spoke of her attachment some years since to Great Britain, and her disposition to assist us. But that moment, he said was past and gone; we had lost it by our own want of exertion, and the Empress was no longer friendly. She neither was willing, nor if she had it in her inclination, was it in her power to afford us effectual and decisive assistance...

Mr. Wraxall proceeded in his picture, and after observing that Poland, Sardinia, Naples and Portugal were only kingdoms in name and therefore of little consideration in a matter of such vast importance, came to his ultimatum, laying it down as a fair conclusion, from what he had said of Denmark, Sweden and Russia, that it was either from Prussia, or Austria, that we must derive assistance.

A LETTER FROM SOUTH CAROLINA, REPORTING ON PRESENT LOCAL SITUATION
March 30, 1781

Charlestown, 1st of January 1781.

I was hopeful, long before this, to have acquainted you with the enjoyments we were once more experiencing under the mild influence of Civil Government; but am sorry to say our country still remains in a very distracted situation, and will continue so, until that desirable event takes place.

I have weathered out a very sickly season, in the course of which there has been the greatest mortality ever known in this country, occasioned by a kind of infectious disorder, which the doctors at length defined to be a species of the yellow fever. It proved a mere plague among the Negroes, sweeping off whole gangs of them at a time; in short, what with pestilence, famine, battle and murder, (all of which we had to encounter) this country has been so much afflicted and impoverished that thirty years, with peace and good government combined, will hardly re-establish it on the flourishing and prosperous footing which it enjoyed at the commencement of the trouble. However, after undergoing the horrors and calamities of war, we may, perhaps, think ourselves blessed, and contented with one half of the enjoyments kind Heaven formerly bestowed upon us, although we were then little sensible of them.

CORNWALLIS REPORTS TO GERMAIN ON DEFEAT AT COWPENS, THE
FOLLOW-UP AND BRITISH VICTORY AT GUILFORD COURTHOUSE
(EXCERPTS)
June 6, 1781

The unfortunate affair of the 17th of January was a very unexpected
and severe blow; however, being thoroughly sensible, that defensive
measures would be certain ruin to the affairs of Britain in the Southern
Colonies, this event did not deter me from prosecuting the original plan.

That General Greene might be uncertain of my intended route as
long as possible, I had left General Leslie at Camden, until I was ready to
move from Wynnesborough, and he was now within a march of me. I
employed the 18th in forming a junction with him, and in collecting the
remains of Lieutenant-Colonel Tarleton's corps; after which great exertions were made by part of the army, without baggage, to retake our
prisoners and to intercept General Morgan's corps, on its retreat to the
Catawba; but the celerity of their movements, and the swelling of the
numberless creeks in our way, rendered all our efforts fruitless...

I had information from our friends who crossed in canoes, that
General Greene's army was marching with the utmost dispatch to form a
junction with him at Guildford. Not having had time to collect the North
Carolina Militia, and having received no reinforcement from Virginia, I
concluded that he would do everything in his power to avoid an action on
the south side of the Dan; and it being my interest to force him to fight, I
made great expedition, and got between him and the Upper Fords; and
being assured that the Lower Fords are seldom practicable in winter, and
that he could not collect many flats at any of the ferries, I was in great
hopes that he would not escape me without receiving a blow.

Nothing could exceed the patience and alacrity of the officers and
soldiers, under every species of hardship and fatigue, in endeavouring to
overtake him; but our intelligence upon this occasion was exceedingly
defective, which, with heavy rains, bad roads, and the passage of many
deep creeks, and bridges destroyed by the enemy's light troops, rendered
all our exertions vain; for upon our arrival at Boyd's Ferry, on the 15th,
we learned that his rear guard had got over the night before, his baggage
and main body having passed the preceding day, at that and a neighbouring ferry, where most flats had been collected than had been represented to me as possible. My force being ill suited to enter by that quarter so powerful a province as Virginia, and North Carolina being in the
utmost confusions, after giving the troops a halt of one day, I proceeded
by easy marches, to Hillsborough, where I erected the King's standard,
and invited, by proclamation, all loyal subjects to repair to it, and to
stand forth and take an active part in assisting me to restore order and
constitutional government. As a considerable body of friends were said
to reside between the Haw and Deept Rivers, I detached Lieut. Col. Tarleton on the 23d, with the cavalry and a small body of infantry, to prevent
their being interrupted in assembling. Unluckily a detachment of the
rebel light troops had crossed the same day, and by accident fell in with
about two hundred of our friends, under Col. Pyle, on their way to Hillsborough, who mistaking the rebels for Lieut. Col. Tarleton's corps, allowed themselves to be surrounded, and a number of them were most

inhumanly butchered, when begging for quarter, without making the least resistance. The same day I had certain intelligence that Gen. Greene having been reinforced, had recrossed the Dan, which rendering it imprudent to separate my corps, occasioned the recall of Lieutenant-Colonel Tarleton's detachment; and forage and provisions being scarce in the neighbourhood of Hillsborough, as well as the position too distant (upon the approach of the rebel army) for the protection of the body of our friends, I judged it expedient to cross the Haw, and encamped near Allamance Creek, detaching Lieutenant-Colonel Tarleton, with the cavalry, light company of the guards, and 150 men of Lieutenant-Colonel Webster's brigade, a few miles from me on the road to Deep River, more effectually to cover the country...

Guildford, March 17, 1781.

I have the satisfaction to inform your Lordship, that his Majesty's troops, under my command, obtained a signal victory, on the 15th instant, over the rebel army, commanded by General Greene.

A PROCLAMATION BY CORNWALLIS
June 6, 1781

Whereas, by the blessing of Almighty God, his Majesty's arms have been crowned with signal success, by the complete victory obtained over the Rebel forces on the 15th instant, I have thought proper to issue this Proclamation, to call upon all loyal subjects to stand forth, and take an active part in restoring good order and government; and whereas it has been represented to me, that many persons in this province who have taken a share in this unnatural rebellion, but having experienced the oppression and injustice of the Rebel Government, and having seen the errors into which they have been deluded by falsehoods and misrepresentations, are sincerely desirous of returning to their duty and allegiance, I do hereby notify and promise to all such persons (murderers excepted) that if they will surrender themselves with their arms and ammunition, at head quarters, or to the officer commanding in the district contiguous to their respective places of residence, on or before the 20th day of April next, they will be permitted to return to their homes, upon giving a military parole; and shall be protected in their persons and properties from all sort of violence from the British troops; and will be restored, as soon as possible, to all the privileges of legal and constitutional government.

Cornwallis

MR. FOX'S MOTION ON THE AMERICAN WAR IN THE HOUSE OF COMMONS, FOLLOWED BY SOME RESPONSES (EXCERPTS)
June 13, 1781

Mr. FOX began with remarking...that the House had not gone so deeply into the discussion of that accursed War and its consequences, as he conceived was necessary; add to which, circumstances had since taken place in America, which materially altered the State of the Question, and rendered it a matter of the first importance, to have the subject again brought under the Consideration of Parliament. Mr. Fox then produced the Gazette, containing Lord Cornwallis's last dispatches, and, with his usual ability, commented on every passage, deducing from the whole a variety of arguments to prove, that according to the noble Lord's information, it was evident the recovery of America by conquest was a matter no longer in the least degree probable. That the noble Lord, in the plainest manner, and by the evidence of facts that had fallen within his own knowledge, showed that all the assertions which had so often been made in that House, that we had a considerable majority of Americans in our favour, especially in the southern Provinces, were utterly false and groundless. That the assertions that the inhabitants of those Provinces were easy of conquest, being, from the nature of the climate, weak, enervated, and less full of spirit than the more northern residents, were likewise false, and in short, that every idea of the war's being likely to be soon ended by a southern campaign, was absurd, ill-founded, ridiculous and improbable...He said it was true, Lord Cornwallis (on whose abilities, valour and good conduct, he passed the warmest eulogium) had gained a victory at Guildford, but then that victory had been attended with all the consequences of a defeat, for he believed it was not to be paralleled in history, that the victors had ever before been under a necessity of retreating and yet such did Lord Cornwallis state to be his situation, and that of the troops under his command...No man would venture to say, his moving that the House resolve itself into a Committee to consider of the American way, would be either a premature, a frivolous, or an improper measure. It might possibly be asked, when the House has resolved itself into a Committee, what do you mean to move next? Would you move that Great Britain grant Independance to America! Undoubtedly he would not. Perhaps it might be right for this country to grant Independance to America. He would not, however, make any such motion, unless he was certain this country would obtain some signal advantage or benefit to balance in its favour against the benefit and advantage America would receive from having Independence ratified by the sanction of the British Parliament. He would fairly say what he meant to do in the Committee. He meant first to promote an Enquiry into the state of the American war, and if it should appear, as he believed and was convinced it would appear, that the war was impracticable, that it had no object, that it was a war of cruelty to America, of ruin to this country; he would then move a resolution to address his Majesty, humbly to beseech him to give instructions to his Ministers to pursue such measures, and such measures only, as were likely to produce conciliation and peace between Great Britain and America.

Mr. Fox...concluded with moving "that the House resolve itself into a Committee to consider of the American war." And he added that if they went into a Committee, he would move there, "that it be a *direction* to his Majesty's Ministers to make peace with America."

Mr. Fox conjured the House to remember, not that they had estates, but that they had constituents. He said, he was old-fashioned enough still to think that ideas of patriotism might in some breasts prevail over those of self-interest.

Lord WESTCOTE rose immediately, and said, he had as much interest in the American war as any gentleman in that House, having lost his best blood in it, but nevertheless he had not changed his opinion respecting it. He had voted for it originally, he had supported it hitherto, and he should still vote for its continuance, and that not from the love he had for war of any kind, much less from a particular zeal for the American war, the expense and inconvenience of which he felt as much as any man; but because he was convinced it could not be put an end to, as matters stood at present, with honour or safety to Great Britain...The American war was in his opinion better deserving of the title of an Holy war, than those wars of olden time, in which all Europe without the slightest provocation sent their thousands and tens of thousands against people in a far distant country and took away the lives of millions who had never given them the slightest offence. Lord Westcote objected to the interference of Parliament on the present occasion, as an unconstitutional invasion of the functions of the executive branch of Government. He said, the Constitution was composed of three distinct powers and descriptions, the monarchy, the aristocracy, and the democracy. The executive branch was lodged in the first - the democracy therefore had no right to assume what was not within their province. His Lordship declared he should for these and other reasons, vote against the Motion.

Sir Thomas CLARGET said, he had given a vote that Session in favour of the American war, but he now meant to vote in a manner directly the reverse. The reason which had induced him to vote in support of the war, was his reliance on the wisdom of Ministers, and on their ability, added to his having been induced to believe that the war was not only practicable, but that our success was certain, and that peace was near at hand. He had now found that those hopes were fallacious, that Ministers were not to be looked up to either for ability or firmness, and the dispatches of Lord Cornwallis had put an end to every expectation, he had formed, of the speedy termination of the war; he therefore should vote in support of the motion.

Mr. TOWNSEND warmly animadverted on the idea which Lord Westcote had suggested, that the American war deserved the epithet of *holy*, and with great shrewdness, drew a comparison between that and the crusades of old. They were, he said, wars of superstition, in which knaves planned, and fools acted. In this war the case was similar; wicked men contrived the war, and they persuaded weaker men to support them in the continuance of it...He also answered what Lord Westcote had said of the Democracy's invading the right of the other powers and said, if the Monarchy and Aristocracy attempted to ruin the constitution, the Democracy ought to be thrown in the opposite scale to preserve a just balance of power.

Sir Edward ASHLEY said, he had lost a son in the American war, as well as the noble Lord who had spoken second in the debate. He had three more sons in the army, and therefore, although he had often given hints to Ministers, respecting the impolicy, cruelty, and ruin of the war, which they had uniformly treated with the most sovereign contempt, he thought he had a right to call upon them to know how many more sons of his they intended to sacrifice, and he would add a hint which, however unpalatable Administration might find it, was founded in truth; it was this: such was our present situation with America, that they must either make peace with her, or demand a truce.

Mr. RIGBY...With regard to the American War, he longed for the conclusion of it as ardently as his Hon. friend, and from the experience of its mischievous consequences which he felt from day to day in his double capacity, as a man in office, and a Member of that House, he did assure his Hon. friend he was most heartily tired of it. At the same time, however, he must of necessity vote against the Motion, and that for this reason; if it were carried, he was convinced that the Motion his Honourable friend had declared, he meant to follow it with, would rather serve to lengthen the War, than to accelerate its issue. It would give nerve and animation to the Americans, and would encourage them to continue the war with greater vigour, under the idea that the British Parliament had declared itself averse to it, and the consequent conclusion, so natural for America to draw, viz. that the people of Great Britain would not much longer endure the continuance of a war which the British Parliament has reprobated.

Lord John CAVENDISH vindicated one of his votes respecting America, and declared he was always for a free dominion. If therefore America could not be happy and enjoy the rights of freedom without independence, he certainly should be for her being independent.

Lord George GERMAIN complimented Mr. Fox on the candour which always distinguished him in every parliamentary step he took...His Lordship then went much at large into the general subject of the American war, justifying its commencement and continuance on the grounds of necessity, expediency and sound policy, and showing the impossibility of pacification at present, with any prospect of safety or honour to Great Britain...His Lordship further repeated what he had formerly said, respecting the great number of loyalists now in the southern provinces, and assigned various reasons in proof of the difficulty and danger of their avowing themselves. He deduced arguments in support of his assertion, from the dispatches of Lord Cornwallis, whence it appeared that General Green drew his resources both of men and provisions from behind him, and not from the southern provinces. He mentioned the butchery of the 200 loyalists by the Americans, and contrasted it with the mild and merciful conduct of Lord Cornwallis, declaring he hoped that examples of lenity would ever distinguish the arms of Great Britain, in equal proportion as those of the Americans were marked with bloodshed and murder. In answer to the charge of his having deceived Lord Cornwallis and given him improper instructions, he must say if there was any deceit in the case, the deceit was mutual. For the information he had given that House relative to the number of loyalists in America, and the proceedings grounded upon that information with regard to the conduct of the war in America, arose entirely from the advices sent over to him by Lord Cornwallis. His Lordship added a great many other arguments, and said he wished for peace with America most sincerely, but till that peace could be had with honour to this country, he must necessarily vote for the continuance of the war, expensive as it was.

Sir George SAVITZ answered Lord George, and opposed arguments of his own those of the noble Lord. Sir George also adverted to the loan and imputed the votes given in support of the American war, to the influence created by corruption.

Mr. Charles DUNDAS supported the motion and declared himself an enemy to the further prosecution of the American war.

General BURGOYNE declared the people here both within doors and without, were miserably deceived respecting America...The General went into a recapitulation of the history of his campaign in America, declaring that no man could go out with more zeal in the service of his country, and that in consequence he did his best, but when he came there, he found he had been greatly deceived respecting the dispositions of the Americans, and their power of procuring provisions, recruits, etc. The General warmly supported the motion.

Mr. ADAM spoke very ably against the motion. He took new ground, as it were. He proved from history, that whenever Parliament had interfered, and snatched the executive powers of Government out of the hands of Ministers, embarrassment and ill success were the certain consequences.

The Lord Advocate spoke long and warmly against the motion. The learned Lord replied to a great variety of arguments which had fallen from different Gentlemen in the course of the debate. He also adduced the language of the late Earl of Chatham, in a famous speech made a little before his death in the House of Lords, in which the noble Earl had declared himself an enemy to the idea of allowing American independency. That declaration, the learned Lord rested on, as a proof that the greatest and most deserved object of public admiration, had given a decisive opinion against allowing independency to America, and he deduced various arguments from it, all of which tended to show the impolicy of that motion, to which the present was barely, but avowedly, a leading one. His Lordship also dwelt, for a considerable time, on the impropriety of Parliament's interfering in matters of war and peace, declaring it was a circumstance unparalleled in our annals.

Mr. PITT rose and very elegantly explained his father's sentiments, asserting that he was an enemy to the American war, though he was desirous that Great Britain should maintain its Sovereignty over the Colonies. He stated, that his father had declared himself adverse to the idea of exercising the right of taxation over America, but that he had advised the withdrawing of the troops from that country. Mr. Pitt, after doing justice to his father, declared his own political creed, and particularly stated that he was from principle an enemy to that cruel, oppressive and ruinous measure the American war, a war which he declared had, in the course of debate, repeatedly, with the strictest propriety, been termed an *accursed* war.

At length Mr. FOX rose again, and made one of the best replies ever made in Parliament. He took notice of the Crusades of old and said those wars ended when Jerusalem was yielded to the Christians, but now, although the sole object of the American war was given up and abandoned, still this country pursued that war with most unrelenting malice. He attacked the Lord Advocate for saying there was no instance in our History of Parliament's having interfered in matters of War and Peace, and instanced the Address of the House of Commons to Queen Anne, beseeching her Majesty not to make peace with Spain, as long as Spain remained in the hands of any branch of the House of Bourbon. He attacked the Lord Advocate also, for quoting detached passages of Lord

Chatham's dying words, without giving at the same time the connecting sequences which explained the whole, and gave it a very different meaning from what it bore when viewed through the medium of a few words, culled for the purpose of the Argument.

Mr. Fox said, the noble Lord at the head of the American department had declared, he wished for peace, but nevertheless he had objected to his motion, which would lead to peace. He desired to know what sort of a peace the noble Lord wanted? He said, the faces of the opposite Bench were full of doubt, confusion, and despair. He hoped, therefore, necessity would oblige them to make peace. He impressed it also upon the House, that we were now continuing the war without an object. The right of taxation had been, long since, given up; the conciliatory propositions did away all that we had been fighting for, and the commission of 1778 gave up, at once, the sovereignty of Parliament.

He concluded with saying he had done his duty by making the motion, and therefore he should leave it to its fate.

At Half past Eleven the House divided, Ayes 99, Noes 172.

PART OF A LETTER ON THE MISCHIEF OF THE BRITISH IN THE AMERICAN WAR
July 5, 1781

The dissipation and unexampled inactivity of the British army, and the unnecessary (waite or waste) of national supplies are universally known in America. The loyalists both within and without the British lines lament all this in vain. The rebels see it with exultation and joy. That these things may be, as well known to Britons as they are to Americans, is absolutely necessary to the safety of the Empire. And it is from a full conviction of this truth, and that the General however well disposed, does not possess abilities equal to the arduous business of so great a command, and from no other motive, that I have taken up the pen.

Nor am I single in this opinion. There are thousands in this kingdom, who think as I do. Indeed it is impossible for any man of candour and enquiry to do otherwise. For we have seen during the last six years from twelve to twenty millions annually granted by the Commons; the most judicious plans laid by the C-b-t, and astonishing exertions by the servants of the Crown, to enable our Generals in America to carry on the war with vigor and success. We have seen our force in America both at sea and on land, vastly superior in numbers, discipline, and appointments, and yet no one campaign has been conducted with vigor, nor anything done towards reducing the rebellion, except by the few troops under Lord Cornwallis. And further we have seen, what was never seen before, our force for the most part of the last three years, sleeping in a garrison, besieged by an enemy greatly inferior both in numbers and discipline. Now under such circumstances, what is to be done? Is the war in America to be carried on in the same indolent manner for six years longer? Are we to supply their extravagance, and to lavish millions upon millions to make Nabobs of all the officers in the departments of the Quartermaster Generals, Commissary Generals, Chief-Engineer, etc., etc.? Surely this cannot be the sense of Britons. All must unite in declaring, that a remedy to these increasing mischiefs - mischiefs which are

54

too heavy to be borne much longer, is absolutely necessary; and that the remedy must arise from giving the chief command to a General, well versed in the science of war, one of approved integrity and spirit, and who prefers the honor and interest of his Sovereign and Country, to every other consideration. It is happy for the nation, that Lord Cornwallis is such a General, and that he is already on the spot.

LETTER FROM JOHN HANCOCK TO GENERAL WASHINGTON
PUBLISHED IN *THE ROYAL GAZETTE*
July 6, 1781

Sir, I received your two letters; and that your sentiments might be as fully conveyed to Congress as they are to me, I sent copies of both to each Member, which as the subject was of such nature as to make its general publication dangerous to the States, we had a private meeting to consider of.

After recapitulating your conduct since you were vested with command, and minutely examining the motives that induced you to take up arms in defence of your country, we must readily acquit you of any sinister design, any selfish view, or any treasonable intention. You have, as a General, acted with a prudent caution, and avoided any decisive action with the enemy. This undoubtedly was our original plan; and you have well executed it; If there were any opportunities which might have gained an advantage for the army of the States, and which offer themselves in the want of Generalship in the enemy, such opportunities being omitted, are not chargeable to your account.

We recollect the strict injunctions you had not to risk a battle, and we console ourselves in the loss of a few advantages, by your many escapes from danger, when an attack by the enemy might have finally put an end to all our hopes. These escapes, Sir, we attribute as well to your military skill as to the hand of providence.

Hitherto we have been distinguished by many marks of Providence in our favour. We have now the assistance of two great allies, from whose interposition we had but very faint hopes at the beginning of the war. Those nations have taken a decided part in our favour; and as it was the world's opinion that in the last war between the House of Bourbon and the House of Hanover, America was the ally that turned the scale in favour of Great Britain, so are we now to hope that she will preponderate with equal weight on the side of France and Spain. To talk therefore of making a submission is to talk idly. We are now a match for our haughty enemy; they know it, they dread it, and the language of some persons speak it.

You say that our finances are low, and our paper money not current; that the troops are discontented, and in some parts almost famishing; you likewise tell us of innumerable desertions, and that the disaffected are many.

All these, Mr. Washington, may be true, and it is what we are to expect. But Great Britain herself has dissatisfied men in her army, her navy and her senate. We have convincing proofs every day of a kindling rebellion in the very heart of that proud Empire. Trust me, Mr. Washington, Heaven has great things yet in store for us; and with such a prospect it is blasphemy against the cause we fight in, to utter a distrust of Providence. As to our credit being low, so is that of England. Our paper currency is as good as their stocks. The value of either is ideal, and the only difference lies in long custom having established English faith, and want of time to prove American punctuality having raised suspicions of our honesty. We should therefore, by every stratagem, keep up the spirits of the people; their despondence alone can do credit an injury.

Disaffection is dangerous, and therefore, by severity in punishment, should be stopped. A few examples always deter the herd; and if you practise, you will find good consequences in the advice. As to deserters, if they do not go over to the enemy, it is only an inconvenience pro tempore; we generally get them again, either as recruits, or by proclamation of pardon. But, Sir, you surprize us in saying the troops are famished. The ratio of provision is regularly paid for, and our contractors are honest men. There surely must be some mistake in that part of your letter, or the complaints made to you are without foundation; however, an enquiry into that supposed grievance shall instantly be made, and I can pledge myself to you, in the name of Congress, that the cause, if any, shall be immediately done away.

The last dispatches we had from Dr. Franklin speak highly of the honourable mention in which the army under your command is made throughout the French dominions; and he gives us every assurance, that so soon as the Channel fleet of Britain is blocked up in Portsmouth, and that Rodney is defeated in the West Indies, a reinforcement of both men and money will be sent to America. The great superiority of the House of Bourbon at sea gives them an authority to talk in high terms of doing as they please with the British fleet. Indeed the navy of England cannot thrive so fast now as it did last war; for every difficulty that the ingenious devices of some persons there can form is daily practised to prevent the First Lord of the Admiralty from doing his business. Not that this is done more to serve us, than it is from the avowed hatred which some persons bear that nobleman; an hatred which will never cease, as it arises from that strong passion jealousy. We may therefore hope in a short time to see the fleet of England moulder away; and then, without any internal commotions, her sun of glory is set for ever.

The melancholy contour of your letter has much affected us all. We know your abilities, and have a strong confidence in them; you are loved and adored by the army; and even your enemies allow you merit. If you desert us it may do us essential mischief; The English consider you as our sheet-anchor; and your resignation would indeed be a triumph to them; you must not therefore at this time think of it; the very idea is dangerous, and if published would sow discontent indeed throughout the army. Lucrative motives, we are certain, are no objects to you, or you might name your terms. The gratitude of America is, however, superior to the promises of Congress; and when the day of peace comes, her glorious General will not be forgot.

As to the conquest of Charles Town it is indeed an immense loss to us; but the victory of Britain in Carolina will be short-lived; we have friends who are working such a mine as will blow up all their triumphal schemes; and if Providence favour us, the news of the surrender will come to their ears a day too late for their rejoicing in London. I have already given you a hint that must raise your expectations. - the explanation will surprize you. (Here follow about 10 lines of strange figures, somewhat like Hebrew characters.)

In a stedfast hope that the God of battles will direct you how best to act, should Clinton attack you, I remain your invariable friend,

J. Hancock

LETTER FROM WASHINGTON TO HANCOCK
PUBLISHED IN *THE ROYAL GEORGIA GAZETTE*, MARCH 22
July 17, 1781

You are to inform Congress, that I received the honour of their letter of the 16th, but that my resolution, if not finally fixed before, is now in fact determined. The surrender of Charlestown explains every doubt.

Tell them, Sir, that whilst I was supported with even the most distant prospect of success, my life, and all I held dear, was at their service. Tell them, I acted from no mean views, from no private purpose. My sentiments were open and candid, as they were constantly delivered. I said, I would hold my services to my country a duty, whilst there were uprightness in the cause, and unanimity in the people; sorry am I now to say, that tyranny is substituted for freedom in the magistrate; and that defection outsoars a love of virtuous liberty in all our troops. I am therefore no longer the commanding officer of the brave citizens, struggling for their rights; I am only a distressed superior among dissatisfied, disaffected complainants whose ardour is cooled, and whose native virtue no longer exists. My troops are tired of war, and destitute of the common comforts of a soldier. I tremble for them when the dreadful day of final derision comes on, when they must (for now it is not to be postponed) meet an army flushed with victory, and refreshed with all the necessaries of war.

Tell Congress all these things, and say, I entreat them to reconsider my former letter, and, as they love the peace and future happiness of poor America, to offer an unconditional sheath to the British sword. Generous even in the hour of their brilliant anger, we need not dread the term that the English may insist on. It is their interest now, to seek our amity, as well as our subjection.

Our friends in London are no longer considered the friends of the people. The faction is split, and for one well-wisher we had an England, we have now an hundred enemies. We never had the love of the English since we took up arms; it was only the pernicious voice of faction there that misrepresented matters here. But this is not a time to prove the fatal cause of the present state of affairs.

In the name of God, I then conjure them to give up the contest, and seek in an humble submission that peace which our arms can never restore. We may again be reinstated in tranquility, and whilst we mourn the relatives slain, we will pray that in their deaths all animosity with England may forever lie buried. The thought of the people will soon be turned to industry, and their amity with Great Britain would close the scene of war with France and Spain, the ports of Europe would again be opened.

Do, Sir, represent these matters, and in my name desire that the last letter I sent may again be referred to. It contains such truths, relative to the state of our credit, and the impossibility of carrying on the war, as must convince, if seriously attended to.

I pray God to direct the resolves of Congress for the best, and that they may with my eyes see inevitable destruction to America in a shameful and total overthrow of her army, if the voice of peace does not immediately stop the victorious troops of Britain.

Washington

FIRST PART OF "ARTICLES OF CAPITULATION" OF THE PROVINCE OF WEST FLORIDA, BETWEEN SPAIN'S MAJOR GENERAL DON BERNADO DE GALVEZ AND BRITAIN'S GOVERNOR PETER CHESTER AND MAJOR-GENERAL JOHN CAMPBELL
August 11, 1781

All the forts and posts now in the possession of the troops of his Britanic Majesty shall (upon a time agreed upon) be delivered up to the troops of his Catholic Majesty. The British garrisons, including soldiers and seamen, to march out with all the honour of war...to the distance of five hundred yards from their respective posts, where they will pile up their arms, officers only reserving their swords, after which they shall be embarked as speedily as possible on board of vessels, provided and sufficiently victualled at the expence of his Catholic Majesty, to be sent as speedily as possible, and without unnecessary delay, to one of the ports belonging to Great Britain, at the option of Major-General Campbell, the men to be under the immediate direction of their own respective officers, and not to serve against Spain or her allies, until an equal number of prisoners belonging to Spain or her allies, shall be given by Great Britain in exchange, according to the established custom of equality of rank, or equivalent thereto.

Granted.-- The ports of St. Augustine and the island of Jamaica only excepted; and as to the punctillio of exchange of prisoners, Spaniards shall be preferred to their allies; the transportation of those who shall be sent to the Spanish ports in exchange, at the expence of his Britanic Majesty.

CLINTON'S PROCLAMATION
August 11, 1781

WHEREAS there are several deserters from the British and foreign troops under my command, who are serving with the enemy, or are concealed in the rebel country, I have thought fit to issue this my proclamation, offering a free and unlimited pardon to all such deserters who shall surrender themselves to any of his Majesty's troops before the 1st day of June next.

And whereas there are many of his Majesty's European subjects serving in the rebel army against their King and country, who stung with remorse, and sensible of the heinousness of such an unnatural proceeding, would be anxious to return to their allegiance, did not their demerits before their arrival in America, make them doubtful of meeting with protection and support within these lines. I do therefore hereby promise all such who shall come in before the above-mentioned 1st day of June 1781, in addition to the benefits, protection, and support, to which they would be entitled under any other proclamation, to procure for them his Majesty's most gracious pardon, for all felonies and treasons (murder excepted) which they have heretofore been guilty of, provided they will take up arms in his service, and give their assistance to the quelling this unnatural rebellion against his government.

VIOLENT REBELS IN NORTH CAROLINA FROM *THE CAPE FEAR NORTH CAROLINA JOURNAL*, JUNE 7, 1781
August 11, 1781

The repeated barbarism of the rebel parties must justify any severities that may in future (and will soon probably) be inflicted on the deluded wretches that compose them; who, under the pretence of patriotism and defence of their country's liberties, assemble to plunder and commit every devastation the mad lawless and unprincipled desire of benefitting themselves, at the expence of their brethren and fellow subjects, can induce.

It is as true as singular, that the most violent men in this part of the country possess little or no property and continue to act against His Majesty's government, solely with a view to benefit themselves in the general confusion, their unprincipled conduct must naturally occasion. We beg leave to instance Mr. John Walker, Thomas Jones, Edmund Corbin, Y---g and many other violent and arch rebels.

OBSERVATION OF A CORRESPONDENT
October 31, 1781

The correspondent observes that future ages will read, with admiration, the history of the present war, notwithstanding in what manner it ends. One half of Europe engaged in supporting the American rebellion, and the other half looking silently on, while the two small islands of Britain and Ireland are without a single ally. What vast commotions have been formed against us! what mighty preparations made to subdue us! and yet our successes have been hitherto as great as if we had but one enemy to cope with. There must always be a reasonable hope of success while the injured party acts only from motives of justice; and here it is necessary to observe, that our modern patriots, who oppose every measure of Government, seem to be the most arrant fools that ever existed; for under the pretence of supporting our liberties at home, they are striving to dismember the British empire, and bring us under the arbitrary power of a foreign yoke.

LETTERS FROM CLINTON TO GERMAIN, DATED SEPTEMBER 12, 1781,
AND SEPTEMBER 26, 1781 (EXCERPTS)
November 7, 1781

New York, September 12, 1781.
I have the honour to inform your Lordship, that the expedition I had
sent against New London is returned, after having destroyed all the
shipping there (except about sixteen, which made their escape up the
river) and an immense quantity of naval stores, European manufactures,
and East and West-India commodities. It gives me concern, however,
that in doing this important service the town was unavoidably burnt,
occasioned by the explosions of great quantities of gunpowder, which
happened to be in the storehouses that were set fire to. Brigadier General Arnold's report with a return of the killed and wounded are enclosed.

New York, September 26, 1781.
I received a letter from the Admiral, dated the 9th instant, to inform
me, that the enemy being absolute masters of the navigation of the
Chesapeak, there was little probability of anything getting into York River
but by night, and an infinite risk to any supplies sent by water; at the
same time acquainting me, that he had on the 5th a partial action with
the French fleet of 24 sail of the line, and that the two fleets had been in
fight of each other ever since; which making it inexpedient to send of the
reinforcement immediately, under such dangerous circumstances, I
thought it right to call a Council of the General Officers on the subject,
who unanimously concurred with me in opinion, that it was most ad-
viseable to wait until more favourable accounts from Rear Admiral
Graves, or the arrival of Admiral Digby, rendered the sailing of the reinforcement less hazardous; but our fleet having arrived at the Hook on the
19th, a Council of War, composed of the Flag and General Officers, was
assembled as soon as possible, the minutes of which will inform your
Lordship, that the exertions of both fleet and army shall be made to form
a junction with the squadron and army in Virginia; Rear Admiral Digby
arrived off the Hook the 24th instant.

A CORRESPONDENT'S OBSERVATION ON GENERAL ARNOLD
November 7, 1781

A correspondent observes, that whatever success may attend General Arnold's operations, his spirited conduct in the late attack of the
American forts, shows him to be well qualified for conducting the most
hazardous undertakings. But what will those in succeeding ages think,
when they read, that a man who was once an enemy to, and actually
bore arms against the forces of his native country, was, after being
brought to a sense of his duty, vilified and traduced by men whose duty
it was to have joined with every loyal subject in bestowing upon him
those honours to which his merits entitled him? But there are too many
examples of this in the history of mankind. Miltiades, Themistocles, and
Acibiades, are well known, and so is the unfortunate Hannibal.

NEWSPAPER REPORTS ABOUT THE PRINCE BRINGING AN OLIVE
BRANCH TO AMERICA, TAXES, RUMORS ABOUT FRANKLIN AND
OBSERVATIONS ON THE HUMAN NATURE OF VARIOUS NATIONS
November 7, 1781

The safe arrival of our gallant young Prince at New York, may be
attended with very salutary and very beneficial consequences, especially
when it is compared with some passages of a similar nature, recorded in
history. The arrival of the amiable prince in America, with the olive
branch in his hand, may operate more vigorously on the minds of the
stubborn, rebellious inhabitants of that country, than the most powerful
armies. However, this much is certain, that although the American
leaders, from motives of conscious guilt, may continue refractory, yet the
general wish of the people is to enjoy peace under the protection of Britain. There is no agreement between the American leaders and the
common people, and there can be little doubt but the latter will in the
end prevail.

A morning paper says, it is very confidently asserted, that Sir Henry
Clinton has transmitted propositions of accommodations from the Congress to Great Britain, and that the following are some of the conditions,
that America shall be at liberty to export certain articles to whatever
country she thinks proper; that she will not export any article from any
other country which Great Britain can supply her with; that all the
internal taxes shall be laid on by the Provincial Assembly, or Continental
Congress, but shall not be effectual without the consent of Great Britain;
that his Majesty shall have the power of stationing the troops, but the
number to be limited by Congress and to be paid by vote of assembly
annually, as in Britain; and that the Parliament of Great Britain shall
have no power to lay on any internal taxes of any kind. These propositions are to be communicated to Parliament at first meeting.

A daily paper asserts that information has been received from Paris
that Doctor Franklin has resigned his public situation there, as Plenipotentiary for the United States of America.

A correspondent who was present a few evenings ago, where the
subject turned upon the nature of humane politeness, it was observed
that the French were polite, the Dutch brutish, the Spaniards proud, the
Italians effiminate, and the Germans blunt and honest. Upon a further
investigation on the subject, it was agreed that the English exceed all
others in the world in honest simplicity, and real gentleness of manners.
Of this we have daily instances, and the humanity of the English exceeds
anything to be met with on the continent of Europe.

"Their generous discord with the battle ends." Our enemies have felt
their wants relieved by our generosity, and our philanthrophy has often
triumphed over mean vulgar prejudices. Let particular vices be ever so
predominant amongst us; we have virtues sufficient to counterbalance
them.

A CORRESPONDENT'S VIEW OF AMERICA; WHO IS COMMANDER OF THE ENGLISH FLEET? WASHINGTON'S ARMY TAKES A NEW POSITION, WASHINGTON TELLS CORNWALLIS TO SURRENDER
November 20, 1781

A correspondent remarks that whatever may be the fate of our army and navy in America, now that things are apparently brought to a crisis, yet the Colonists will still be the losers, and their eyes will be opened to see their folly at a period of time when it will be too late for them to retract. Should the French prevail, the Americans, who have long boasted of nominal liberty, will become slaves to arbitrary power, and the liberty of conscience they now enjoy, with respect to religion, will be annihilated, and mass will be celebrated in their meetings; They refused to pay small taxes to the mother country, and treated the Custom-house officers in the most barbarous manner; but the French will not be at the trouble to tar and feather the hypocritical Americans, for they will dragoon them into payment, as they did in France after the revocation of the edict of Nantz.

The public seem at present not to know for certain, who is the commander of our fleet in the Chesapeak; some accounts have given the command to Admiral Graves, while others have transferred it from him to Admiral Digby; the fact is, that the former has really the supreme command; and the following particulars will explain away the difficulties that may appear to attend this case:

The Cabinet undoubtedly intended that Rear Admiral Digby should be commander in chief on the coast of America; but as Admiral Graves was his senior officer, it became necessary that he should be removed; accordingly, at the same time that Digby's commission was made out, orders were really sent to Graves to sail for the West Indies, where he was appointed commander in chief. Admiral Graves, however, did not receive these orders till the 26th of September; and on that same day Admiral Digby arrived at New York. A difficulty then flarred, who should preside in a council of war, which had been summoned; the presidency belonged to Graves, by seniority; to Digby, by commission; the latter, however, generously prevented any dispute; and preferring the unanimity of the fleet, and consequently the good of the service to the mere pageantry of command, requested that Admiral Graves would still retain the chief command; he said the service on which they were all bound, was critical, and required the greatest abilities to effect it; he therefore begged he would remain with the fleet; and if he should not be inclined to grant his request, he said he would make use of the authority given to him by his commission, to command Admiral Graves to remain at the head of the fleet.

Admiral Graves acquiesced; and the Council was held; and perhaps since the eve of the battle of Agincourt, a more daring resolution, or more worthy of Britons, was never taken than in that council; it was there resolved to sail as soon as possible for the Chesapeak, and with *twenty three ships* of the line, and two fifties, to attack a fleet of *thirty six* line of battle ships.

Baltimore, October 2.

A late letter from Williamsburgh mentions, that the allied army under command of his Excellency General Washington, consisting of upwards of 15,000 effective men, all in health and high spirits, had taken an advantageous position in the neighbourhood of York Town, and would immediately commence very serious operations against this important British post.

Philadelphia, October 5.

By a gentleman who came to town yesterday from Williamsburgh, which place he left on Wednesday the 20th ult. we have the following interesting intelligence, viz. that on the day he left that place, General Washington had summoned Lord Cornwallis to surrender, who replied, "he would defend the post while he had a man left alive;" whereupon General Washington immediately gave orders for the heavy cannon to play upon his Lordship - this began about ten o'clock in the morning, and continued unremittedly, till near eleven at night, by which time the allied forces had gained three of the enemy's redoubts.

CORNWALLIS'S LETTER TO CLINTON, DESCRIBING HIS SITUATION AS BEING CRITICAL, DATED OCTOBER 15, 1781
November 28, 1781

Last evening the enemy carried my two advanced redoubts on the left by storm, and during the night have included them in their second parallel, which they are at present busy in perfecting.

My situation now becomes very critical. We dare not shew a gun to their old batteries, and I expect the new ones will be open to-morrow morning. Experience has shown that our fresh earthen works do not resist their powerful artillery, so that we shall soon be exposed to an assault in ruined works, in a bad position, and with weakened numbers.

The safety of the place is therefore so precarious, that I cannot recommend that the fleet and army should run great risque in endeavouring to save us.

CLINTON'S LETTER TO GERMAIN ABOUT CORNWALLIS'S CAPITULATION AT YORKTOWN, (EXCERPTS) DATED OCTOBER 29, 1781
November 28, 1781

Agreeable to the information which I had the honour to give your Lordship in my last dispatch, the fleet, under the command of Rear Admiral Graves, sailed from Sandy Hook on the 19th instant, and arrived off Cape Charles on the 24th, when we had the mortification to hear that Lord Cornwallis had proposed terms of capitulation to the enemy on the 17th...Since then we have been plying off the Capes, with variable and hard gales of wind, to the present hour, without being able to procure any further information...we cannot entertain the least doubt of his Lordship's having capitulated, and that we are unfortunately too late to relieve him; which being the only object of the expedition, the Admiral has determined upon returning with his fleet to Sandy Hook.

ARTICLES OF CAPITULATION (LISTING ONLY ARTICLE I)
November 28, 1781

Made between his Excellency General Washington, Commander in Chief of the combined forces of America and France, his Excellency the Count de Rochambeau, Lieutenant General of the King of France's armies, Grand Cross of the Royal and Military order of St. Louis, commanding the auxiliary troops of his Most Christian Majesty in America, and his Excellency the Count de Grasse, Lieutenant General of the naval forces of his Most Christian Majesty, Commander of the Order of St. Louis, commanding in chief the naval force of France in the Bay of Chesapeak, on one part; and the Right Honourable, the Earl Cornwallis, Lieutenant General of his Britannic Majesty's forces, Commander of the Garrisons of York and Gloucester, and Thomas Symonds, Esq.; commanding the Naval Forces of his Britannic Majesty, in York River, in Virginia, on the other.

Article I. The garrisons of York and Gloucester, including the officers and sailors of his Britannic Majesty's ships, as also all other seamen, shall surrender themselves prisoners of war, to the combined forces of America and France; the land troops shall be prisoners to the United States; the whole Marine shall be prisoners to the naval forces of his Most Christian Majesty.

ADDRESS OF THE KING (EXCERPTS) TO A SPECIAL GATHERING OF THE HOUSE OF LORDS, WITH AN INVITATION TO THE HOUSE OF COMMONS, AND REPLIES FROM SOME LORDS (EXCERPTS)
November 28, 1781

...In the course of this year, my assiduous endeavour to guard the extensive dominions of my crown have not been attended with success equal to the justice and uprightness of my views; and it is with great concern that I inform you that the events of war have been very unfortunate to my arms in Virginia, having ended in the loss of my forces in that province.

No endeavours have been wanting on my part to extinguish that spirit of rebellion, which our enemies have found means to forment...to my deluded subjects in America that happy and prosperous condition which they formerly derived from a due obedience to the laws; but the late misfortune in that quarter calls loudly for your firm concurrence and assistance, to frustrate the designs of our enemies, equally prejudicial to the real interests of America, and to those of Great Britain.

Gentlemen of the House of Commons,

I will order the estimates for the ensuing year to be laid before you. I rely on your wisdom and public spirit for such supplies as the circumstances of our affairs shall be found to require. Among the many ill consequences which attend the continuation of the present war, I most sincerely regret the additional burthens which it must unavoidably bring upon my faithful subjects.

My Lords, and Gentlemen,

In the prosecution of this great and important contest in which we are engaged, I retain a firm confidence in the protection of Divine Providence, and perfect conviction of the justice of my cause; and I have no doubt but that, by the concurrence and support of my Parliament, by the valour of my fleets and armies, and by a vigorous, animated, and united exertions of the faculties and resources of my people, I shall be enabled to restore the blessing of a safe and honourable peace to all my dominions.

Lord SOUTHHAMPTON in a short speech lamented the loss we had so recently sustained...His Lordship summed up his speech by earnestly exhorting the House to recollect that the eyes of all the world were turned on their Lordships, and that it depended on the proceedings of that day to shew mankind in general that the people of England would not tamely submit to the dismemberment of their empire, but like their Prince possessing true magnanimity of mind, derived fresh ardour from affliction, and that encrease of danger and difficulty only added to the energy of their exertions.

Lord WYCOMB (Earl of Shelbourne)...The Speech and the Address talked of prosecuting the war; - how was it possible? Where were the resources? With regard to men and money, to say nothing of the conduct of the Admiralty, and of the Army and Navy, where were they to be had? From living in the country, he knew that a single recruit for any of the old regiments was scarcely to be obtained on any terms. Our Navy too; if we had the best First Lord of the Admiralty, and the ablest Board that ever sat, it was impossible to provide for all the distant services of so extensive a war; and the reason was obvious, the fine Navy that belonged to Great Britain at the conclusion of the last war had been suffered to rot and moulder away, while France and Spain had been recruiting and repairing their navy, during the whole of the peace. With regard to money, the last loan of twelve millions cost the country twenty-one, so extravagant were the terms on which the money was borrowed! The war had already added eighty millions to the National Debt, and before the next campaign was over it would amount to one hundred, so that in fact, we should have double the interest of the National Debt to pay without the smallest prospect of peace. With regard to allies, where to look for them?

The Duke of RICHMOND...believed that the King's Ministers, and not the restless ambition of his Majesty's enemies, were the cause, not only of the war, but of all the calamities that had followed one another so fast, almost from the commencement of the present reign. We owed the dreadful and disgraceful situation of our affairs to what many a man owed his private misfortunes - to folly...He said it was the duty of their Lordships to suggest salutary advice to the Crown, and to stand up as assertors of the rights of the people, but that he thought there was little prospect of giving that advice with any effect, unless the original principles of the constitution were restored, and particularly the people had a real representation in the other House of Parliament. At present, his Grace said, scarcely a seventh part of the people were represented, while all the remainder had no concern whatever, either virtually or individually in the management of their own affairs, which their Lordships well knew, the constitution of this country, as originally framed, gave them a right to have. He appealed to the House, whether many of their Lordships did not name the members for several boroughs, and whether the representatives were not chosen only by the management of two or three burgesses? Was that the sort of representation designed by the Constitution? Undoubtedly it was not. When this matter was reformed, his Grace declared he should hope to see the country in a way to regain somewhat of its former greatness, but there were several things which he should advise as steps to success equally necessary; and first he would wish Ministers to consider themselves as somebody, and to have a communication with each other; in short, so to act together, and in a manner which should appear to arise from concerted judgement and comparative opinion. At present, he said, the country was governed by Clerks, each Minister standing upon his single footing, and confining himself to his own office; the consequence was, there was no responsibility, no union of opinion, no concerted measures, but in the stead thereof, disunion, weakness, and corruption. The Interior Cabinet, he declared, had been the ruin of this country.

IN THE HOUSE OF COMMONS MR. TOWNSEND BLAMES THE LORD OF THE ADMIRALTY FOR CORNWALLIS'S MISFORTUNE (EXCERPTS)
November 30, 1781

...With regard to the capture of Lord Cornwallis and his brave troops, it was a circumstance to be adverted to with the deepest regret; but in the midst of the general sorrow, there was no one circumstance in his noble and gallant friend's character, that more particularly entitled him to the thanks and gratitude of his countrymen, and pointed him out as a man of singular greatness of mind, than his letter to Sir Henry Clinton, during the siege. Surrounded as he was by the brave troops, the companions of his glory, troops that he loved and regarded as his children, still his wishes for his country's welfare were predominant; and even before he thought of the means of providing for the safety of himself, and those veterans that looked up to him as to a father, he found the means to give vent to his anxiety to save the fleet of that Lord of the Admiralty, whose negligence and misconduct were the cause of his distressed situation. That Lord of the Admiralty, who had disgraced Great Britain, as a naval power, and sacrificed the empire of the sea by his scandalous inattention.

MR. FOX'S STARTLING STATEMENT IN THE HOUSE OF COMMONS (EXCERPTS)
December 3, 1781

Mr. Fox said, the Ministry had incurred this dilemma - their conduct had been such, that they must be deemed either ignorant or criminal. Ignorant in choosing officers that were incapable of executing their plans; or wicked, in knowingly employing incapable officers. But it was sufficient that they had for seven years been unsuccessful; that they ought to retire, or avowedly change their system.

CONTINUING DEBATE ABOUT THE WAR IN THE HOUSE OF COMMONS
(EXCERPTS)
December 13, 1781

Sir James LOWTHER said, the King's Speech had talked of the prosecution of the War, in a manner that had alarmed the whole country;...the Address had pledged the House to the prosecution of the American War; therefore on that account, as well as from a consideration of the melancholy state of our affairs, in consequence of the various calamities of the war, and especially the late dreadful disaster that had befallen Lord Cornwallis in the Chesapeak, he thought it highly incumbent on that House, previous to their voting the army, to come to some solemn resolution, in order to mark and define their idea of the American war, and to convince their constituents, that they were awake to the real state of the country, and anxious to do their duty, in a manner becoming the representatives of a great and a free people. Sir James concluded with reading two motions, to the following effect:

I. That it is the opinion of this House that all our efforts to reduce America to obedience by force, have been ineffectual, and have only tended to weaken this country and exhaust its resources, while they have served to strengthen the hands of our ancient and natural enemies; and

II. That this House is of opinion, that all further efforts to subdue the Americans to obedience by force, will be ineffectual, and injurious to the interest of Great Britain, by tending to weaken our endeavours to resist our ancient and natural enemies.

Mr. POWYS, in one of the ablest speeches he ever made in parliament, supported Sir James Lowther, and seconded the motions. Mr. Powys shortly and pointedly reviewed the disasters of the war, comparing each event with the language of Ministers from time to time, and asking whether our continuing the war with America had served to protect our West India islands from the successful attacks of our ancient foes? After dwelling for some time on this subject, he presented the House with a portrait of a declining empire, from the celebrated work of Mr. Gibbon, and shewed the analogy between the declension of Rome, and the visible declension of Great Britain...Mr. Powys ascribed the long prosecution of the American war solely to the obstinacy of Ministers, and their anxiety to hold their situation. He paid the majority some compliments, declaring he knew they were not the corrupt and venal slaves of the Minister, which some gentlemen had represented them, but that there were among them men who had neither office nor emolument from administration, men who were perfectly honest, disinterested, and independent, and whose support of the measures of Government was founded upon the purest principles! He called upon those gentlemen to step forward at that moment and save their country, for (he declared) on the event of that day depended, not only the crisis of the Session, but the crisis of the British Empire, the fate of which was within a single vote of perdition!

Lord NORTH said...that if the present motions were carried, they would clearly convince the enemy in what manner they might best point their operations against this country during the ensuing campaign...He felt himself bound in some degree, and especially, after what passed lately on another occasion, to speak more out upon the design of the future mode of the prosecution of the war, than he was generally accustomed to do, or indeed than it was either wise or politic for a man in a high and responsible office to do, at any time, unless the urgent necessity of the case rendered it impossible for him to make any other election of conduct; it was from this consideration, that he informed the House, that from the misfortunes and calamities of the war, (both of which he would then and at all times maintain, were misfortunes and calamities, which, tho of a very serious and fatal nature, were matters rather to be deplored and lamented, as the inevitable events of war, ever in themselves uncertain, than to be ascribed to any criminality in Ministers;) yet the misfortunes and calamities of the war rendered it necessary to Government to determine that the mode of carrying on the war internally upon the Continent of America, as had been the practice under Lord Cornwallis and other Generals, should no longer be followed, but to change the form of the war altogether...Mr. Powys had said respecting the war being the war of Ministers, and a war adhered to obstinately by them, as the sole means by which they hold their situation, and whence along they derived all their emoluments, as well as all their power. Those sort of remarks, he observed, had been made again and again, and they had been as often answered and refuted. For the present he should only say, that the war never had been a favourite of his; on the contrary, he had always considered it as a war of the most cruel necessity, but as a war founded on truly British basis; a war, instituted in support of the just rights of the Crown and of the Parliament of Great Britain. In that point of view, and that only, ought the war to be regarded, and in that point of view, he repeated what he had often before said, that the war was, in its origin, just and necessary, however calamitous to the country its events had unfortunately proven.

Lord George GERMAIN...declared he regarded the motions, as amounting to a resolution to abandon the American war altogether, he made no scruple to avow that if the House came into it, he would immediately retire; for be the consequence what it might, he never would be the minister to sign any instrument which gave Independence to America. His opinion ever had been, and his opinion then was that the moment the House acknowledged the Independence of America the British empire was ruined. This nation never could exist as a great and a powerful people, unless our Sovereign was likewise the Sovereign of America.

GENERAL CONWAY'S OPINION IN THE HOUSE OF COMMONS
December 15, 1781

General CONWAY expressed himself not in the least satisfied. He wished the American war to be abandoned altogether, to have every one of our troops withdrawn, and to put an end to it wholly, that the mischief that had already nearly ruined the country, might exist no longer. He said, he considered avowing the Independence of America as a grievous calamity, and a most shameful disgrace to Great Britain; but still, of two evils he would chose the least, and he would submit to the Independence of America, - in short, he would almost submit to anything rather than go on a day longer with the war, if it were possible to get rid of it.

A CORRESPONDENT'S VIEW OF THE STATE OF AFFAIRS
December 15, 1781

A correspondent says, as Britain had never yet such a struggle as at present, with the most formidable foreign enemies, as well as rebel subjects, it will be the admiration of future ages, to read of the manner in which we have been enabled to continue the war. As if the revolt of thirteen colonies had not been sufficient to distress this ancient kingdom, our natural enemies have been brought in as auxiliaries; and our natural allies the Dutch, have been fatally persuaded to take up arms against us. To all this may be added, that notwithstanding our critical situation abroad, yet we are even in a worse condition at home. From the Senate down to the meanest cabal of the lowest miscreant, parties are formed, to traduce the character of those in power; and strange as well as unnatural it may appear, success is wished to American rebellion. Under such a complication of untoward circumstances, great fortitude and unanimity, in a just cause, may give us the most rational hopes of success, and convince the world that Britain is not to be trampled on.

WASHINGTON'S DISPATCH TO CONGRESS REGARDING CORNWALLIS'S SURRENDER AT YORKTOWN (EXCERPTS)
December 22, 1781

Headquarters, October 19, 1781.
I have the honour to inform Congress, that a reduction of the British army under the command of Lord Cornwallis, is most happily effected. The unremitted ardour which actuated every officer and soldier in the combined army on this occasion, has principally led to this important event, at an earlier period than my most sanguine hopes had induced me to expect.

The singular spirit of emulation which animated the whole army from the first commencement of our operations, had filled my mind with the highest pleasure and satisfaction, and had given me the happiest presages of success.

On the 17th instant, a letter was received from Lord Cornwallis, proposing a meeting of Commissioners to consult on terms for the surrender of the posts of York and Gloucester.- This letter (the first that had passed between us) opened a correspondence, a copy of which I do myself the honour to enclose; that correspondence was followed by the definitive capitulation, which was agreed to and signed on the 19th, a copy of which I herewith transmit; and which, I hope, will meet with the approbation of Congress.

I should be wanting in the feelings of gratitude, did I not mention, on this occasion, with the warmest sense of acknowledgements, the very cheerful and able assistance which I have received in the course of our operations, from his Excellency the Count de Rochambeau - Nothing could equal this zeal of our allies, but the imitating spirit of the American officers, whose ardour would not suffer their exertions to be exceeded...

I wish it was in my power to express to Congress, how much I feel myself indebted to the Count de Grasse and the officers of the fleet under his command, for the distinguished aid and support which has been afforded by them, between whom and the army, the most happy concurrence of sentiments and views have subsisted, and from whom every possible co-operation has been experienced, which the most harmonious intercourse could afford...

Your Excellency and Congress will be pleased to accept my congratulations on this happy event...

P.S. Though I am not possessed of the particular returns, yet I have reason to suppose that the number of prisoners will be between five and six thousand, exclusive of seamen and others.

A LETTER FROM A GENTLEMAN IN NEW YORK TO HIS RELATIVE IN LONDON WITH REGARD TO CORNWALLIS, DATED NOVEMBER 1, 1781
December 26, 1781

"With much concern I am to acquaint you, of the taking of Lord Cornwallis, with his brave army, by the French and rebels on the 19th of last month. Never, I believe, was an army so lost, not through any fault of the noble Earl, but entirely owing to our Commander in Chief, for which, I am convinced, he must render an account when he arrives in England. Every person of sense in this city, is highly dissatisfied with Sir H. C. believing he might have prevented this fatal surrender.

I will mention two instances, in which, I presume to think, he might have saved that noble Officer and his army; - Washington with an army of French and rebels, in the summer, lay within a few miles of Kingsbridge. We had at least twelve thousand men in the city and at Kingsbridge, which was near one half more than Washington's army, but our Commander in Chief would not venture to attack them. - Washington on finding this, moved on his way to Virginia through the Jerseys, and lay at Elizabeth-Town, about three days. Many persons in town expected our army would have gone into Jersey, to have stopped him from going against Lord Cornwallis, which at the time, was well known to be Washington's intention; but, to our great sorrow, it was not done, although, if it had been done, Washington's career would have been effectually prevented.

I am informed a certain General, now in the city, offered to go into Jersey, to stop Mr. Washington, but it was not attended to.

The second instance in which I think Lord Cornwallis and his army might have been saved is, his Lordship was obliged to surrender for want of ammunition, which I cannot help thinking was well known here; notwithstanding which, I am informed, that a ship is now in this harbour loaded with all kinds of artillery stores for Lord Cornwallis; and that this ship has been lying here loaded ever since May 1st. Whose fault it is she never sailed, time must discover.

Every loyalist in this city feels very sensibly this heavy loss. How Government will act in consequence of it, is impossible for any person on this side of the Atlantic to form an idea. We in this city wait with much anxiety their determination. - I hope they won't give up this country; Indeed I think they cannot, there being too much depending."

CHAPTER VI

January - March 9, 1782

From
The Morning Chronicle and London Advertiser
(unless otherwise noted)

(All quotations, except headings)

THE KING PROCLAIMS A FAST (EXCERPTS)
January 11, 1782

We, taking into our most serious consideration the just and necessary hostilities in which we are engaged, and the unnatural rebellion carrying on in some of our provinces and colonies in North America, and putting our trust in Almighty God, that he will vouchsafe a special blessing on our arms both by sea and land, have resolved, and do, by and with the advice of our Privy Council, hereby command, that a public Fast and Humiliation be observed throughout that part of our kingdom of Great Britain called England, our dominions of Wales and town of Berwick upon Tweed, upon Friday the 8th day of February next; that so both we and our people may humble ourselves before Almighty God, in order to obtain pardon of our sins; and may, in the most devout and solemn manner, send up our prayers and supplications to the Divine Majesty, for averting those heavy judgments which our manifold sins and provocations have most justly deserved, and imploring his blessing and assistance on our arms and for restoring and perpetuating peace, safety, and prosperity, to us and our kingdom.

A LETTER BY "ANTI-YANKY" (EXCERPTS)
January 22, 1782

The perfidy and inhumanity of the Americans is well known to those whom the fortune of war put into their hands, but particularly so to the unfortunate corps once commanded by the gallant Burgoyne...
I was a prisoner in the hands of the rebels, for above three years, and in writing this, declare that I am not actuated by any motive whatever, than an earnest desire of setting such of my fellow subjects right, who by attending to certain flowery harangues, may be led to believe, that the British arms have been tarnished by a wanton cruelty offered to their prisoners, while the Congress, who have been guilty of actions that

would have disgraced a pillory or a gibbet, are held forth to view by the mercenary orators, "the most glorious Assembly."

What I undertake is by no means difficult. - I am a mere soldier, and shall confine myself to facts that happened within my own knowledge.

When the American Congress thought proper to violate the Convention of Saratoga, and detain our army then quartered in the vicinity of Boston, the cruel and persecuting spirit of the rebels broke forth with its usual violence. Centinels were placed round the barracks at Prospect and Winter Hills, who wantonly fired upon the soldiers wives, who were not permitted to buy necessaries for their families. Our officers and soldiers were daily assaulted and abused without provocation, and no redress could be obtained. Our little hovels were repeatedly ransacked on pretence that we had concealed cannon and military stores!

In short, the slightest occasion were sought for, and every method used, to irritate and provoke our troops to give them a favourable pretence to fire on us. At Length Colonel Henly, the commanding officer of the American escort, with an armed detachment of his troops, marched up to our barracks, and wantonly stabbed several of the British soldiers. The facts were proved at a Court martial (to which the poltroon was brought by General Burgoyne) yet they acquitted the wretch, and reinstated him in his command!

The shocking and deliberate murder of Lieut. Brown of the 21st regiment, and their acquittal of the murderer, will ever stigmatize their country, and remain a horrid proof of their unjust and cowardly dispositions.

But peace to your manes, amiable youth, your death, I trust, will yet be revenged.- For a moment I shall quit the disagreeable recital of our sufferings, and go back to the year 1776. Did not a rebel officer, Lieut. Whitcomb of Connecticut, with a skulking party of five, assassinate in Canada Brigadier General Gordon, who was alone unarmed, and whom they might have taken with the greatest ease?- Yet so far were Congress from discountenancing such actions, that the assassin was shortly after made a Colonel.

CORNWALLIS'S RETURN TO ENGLAND
January 22, 1782

The cause of Lord Cornwallis's leaving America, and his Lordship's arrival in England have been attended with circumstances of a very singular nature. After distinguishing himself as almost the only General Officer, who was really zealous to serve his country in America and, endeavoured by a wise and spirited exertion of the force put under his command, to bring the war to a conclusion, his Lordship felt himself reduced to the cruel necessity, after a series of brilliant successes, of laying down his arms and resigning his gallant army prisoners of war to the superior forces of France and America conjoines; an event, which nothing could have rendered him liable to, but his being most shamefully deserted by those who ought, and who had it in their power to have supported him by a reinforcement, and an event under which, dreadful and degrading to a gallant mind has it must have been, his Lordship conducted himself with the most laudable firmness and wisdom, procuring better terms of capitulation than could reasonably have been expected to have been obtained for an army captured under such circumstances. Lord Cornwallis is permitted to set sail for England, and in his passage he is again made a prisoner, and the vessel in which he was a passenger, is steered toward France. The winds and waves seem conscious of the accumulated ill-fortune of so brave an officer, and such is the effect of the weather, that the transport is shattered, her rigging damaged, and her crew so totally exhausted, that there does not appear the smallest chance of working her into a French port; the only alternative that remains is, that of suffering the vessel to go down, or endeavouring to gain some English harbour. The Captain's interest forbids him to make the latter election, and such we understand is the strange obstinacy and pride of human nature, that the French Lieutenant who had the prize in his care, on board of which Lord Cornwallis and Lord Chewton were, would not consent to accede to turn the ship towards the English coast, till both the noble Lords, actuated by a wish to save the lives of so many souls, pledged their honours to the French officer, that provided he would make instantly for England, they would engage that the vessel should be given up to him, and that they would consider themselves as prisoners on parole, to be disposed of in a future exchange. Such are the extraordinary circumstances under which Lord Cornwallis and Lord Chewton have arrived in England.

A CORRESPONDENT'S OBSERVATION ON AMERICA
January 31, 1782

A correspondent observes, that the longer the war is continued in America, the plainer do the designs of the French appear. It is certain, that the Americans would never have set up for independency, had not they been misled and deluded by a powerful inveterate faction at home. They were made to believe, that the majority of people in this country would join together in their favour, and at last, when they found themselves disappointed, they, in order to complete their pain threw themselves upon the French. This was just what the deceitful, perfidious Monsieur longed for, it was the grand object they had in view, and their success has been equal to their expectations. Wherever their arms have obtained conquests, they have displayed French colours, and celebrated the Roman mass, even in the midst of Presbyterians, who of all others are the most averse to Popery. The Americans must either submit to Britain, or wear the Gallitian chains.

TORY SPIES ARE EXECUTED IN PHILADELPHIA
January 31, 1782

Philadelphia, November 14.
On Thursday morning last, Laurence Marr and John Moody, both of Col. Barton's Tory regiment, were apprehended in this city on suspicion of being spies. On the two following days they were indulged with a candid and full hearing, before a respectable board of officers, whereof the Hon. Major General the Marquis de la Fayette was President. It appeared, their business was to steal and carry off the secret Journals of

Congress, and other papers, to New York. They have made several interesting discoveries of many persons in these States, who are doing their utmost to ruin their country. - The names of these ingrates will appear in proper time. The Board of Officers having reported to the Honourable Board of War, their opinion was approved, and Marr and Moody were both sentenced to die; which sentence was executed on Moody yesterday between the hours of eleven and twelve. Marr is respited until Friday the 23rd instant. From Saturday evening until yesterday, the criminals were both at ended by a gentleman of the clerical order, who gives us ground to hope they were real penitents, as from the beginning of their confinement they manifested the greatest contrition for all their sins, political and moral. - The enemy, who at this period seem equal to no exploits superior to robbing mail and stealing papers, may thank the monster Benedict Arnold, their beloved friend, for the untimely death of this young man, who was only in his 23rd year.

NEWS FROM NEW YORK
January 31, 1782

Chatham, November 21.
By recent advices from New York we learn, that Admiral Graves, with ten ships of the line, has sailed for the West Indies.- That the army have lost all confidence in Sir Henry Clinton, and execrate him as he passes the streets; some go so far as to swear he is a lunatick.- That General Arnold, apprehensive of danger, has obtained liberty to go to England.- That the Tories bitterly bewail their situation, fearing that the "civil resort" will, before long, be their destiny.

A CORRESPONDENT'S VIEW OF THE DUTCH AND AMERICANS
January 31, 1782

A correspondent says, it is now a matter beyond all manner of dispute, that however willing the Dutch might be to make peace with England, yet such is their present situation and circumstances, that they cannot do so without the consent and permission of the French. The French have treated the Dutch in the same manner as they have the Americans. The Dutch and the Americans, by an uniform attachment to a system of hypocrisy and dissimulation, have proved themselves to be the most arrant fools in the world, and indeed it generally happens that those who are otherwise in their own conceits, are taken by surprize in their own craftiness. This is the real state of the Dutch and Americans at present, and nothing less than a sense of that duty they have forsaken can prevent their total ruin.

HOUSE OF LORDS DISCUSSES THE EXECUTION OF THE AMERICAN COLONEL HAYNES (EXCERPTS)
February 5, 1782

From *The Morning Herald and Daily Advertiser*.
The Duke of RICHMOND...said he came before their Lordships with no other authority to support his charge than that which arose from a

letter sent to him by a Mr. Bowen, whom he did not know; and a Pensylvania newspaper, containing a proclamation by General Greene. The subject of that proclamation, indeed, was of a very alarming nature. It threatened those British officers, who might unfortunately become prisoners to the American army, with a retaliation of that cruelty and injustice which were exercised By Lord Rawdon and Colonel Balfour on the person of Mr. Haynes; who as his Grace understood, was put to death in a most unwarrantable, and unsoldier-like manner...

After strongly marking the several stages of Lord Rawdon's and Colonel Balfour's conduct in this affair, his Grace particularly recapitulated the inhumanity of that short time, which those officers gave to the unhappy man to settle his private affairs, and prepare himself for the awful change he was soon to experience. Twenty-four hours respite were, it is true, first granted; and on the strenuous request of the Governor and some of the principal inhabitants of Charlestown, 24 hours more were added to that respite. But the very causes assigned in the latter petition for that further mercy to the unhappy man, appeared so much in his favor, that they ought to have mitigated the punishment to something of a more tender nature, than that of prolonging misery for a few hours. Those causes, his Grace said, were, *that Colonel Haynes had given proofs of the kindest treatment to such British* as were so unfortunate as to become his prisoners of war. Common humanity, therefore, should have operated in favor of the man who himself had exercised that virtue; and evil, in such a case, should not have been returned for good...At present the virtuous character of the British nation was called in question, and its humanity sullied by public report in all foreign courts.

The Duke of MANCHESTER went over part of the same argument, which was adopted by his Grace of Richmond. He condemned the cruelty of executing a man without a trial and much dreaded retaliation on the part of America.

Lord SHELBURNE who took up the matter of the wide field of the American war, which in the most severe and animated terms, he condemned as cruel, unjust, and highly ruinous. His Lordship insisted that everything which lead to an enquiry into our national disgraces, our national calamities, and our national misconduct was not a matter to be done away by logical definition, nor were the ministers to screen the badness of their conduct when enquiry was instituted, merely by parliamentary forms, or the little minutiae of official order. The simple question is this. Have they acted wrong, or has any officer under their instructions acted wrong? If there is no misconduct, why shuffle off an enquiry?-The actions of justice bear the light of investigation. It is infamy alone that seeks the shade.

CONTINUING DISCUSSION ON THE EXECUTION OF COLONEL HAYNES (EXCERPTS)
February 5, 1782

From *The Morning Chronicle.*
The Duke of RICHMOND exhorted the House to consider how the nation was situated at the present moment? - Engaged in an expensive bloody and unsuccessful war with America, and engaged at the same

time with all the maritime powers in Europe almost, excepting only a few of the Northern States. So circumstanced, it behoved us to act carefully and guardedly, and at any rate to avoid introducing now modes of cruelty, unknown in former wars, and such as had never before disgraced the British arms. The execution of Colonel Haynes, without a trial, without an opportunity of making any defence, was, in his opinion, if the facts were stated truly, in that representation of them which he had related, as well as the manner in which he came by that representation, a matter that called seriously upon their Lordships for an Enquiry; by instituting such an Enquiry they would convince their enemies that they neither authorized, nor countenanced cruelty, and that even when a report of any acts of unwarrantable severity having been committed by British officers reached their ears, they immediately set on foot an enquiry, in order to come at the truth...

His Grace moved,

"That an humble Address be presented to his Majesty, humbly to desire, that his Majesty will be graciously pleased to give direction, that there be laid before this House, Copies or Extracts of Letters and Papers (here the Duke read a very long list of the titles of those papers he wished to have presented) relative to the execution of Col. Isaac Haynes, beginning with a copy of the Articles of Capitulation on the reduction of Charlestown by the British arms, and enumerating every instruction sent by Ministers to the officers commanding the Southern army, with Minutes of the Proceedings, and Copies of their Proclamations, down to the period of Mr. Hayne's execution."

Lord SHELBURNE rose next, and declared that he thought the subject of the present debate so important, that he had endeavored to keep his mind clear of any prejudice...Though he had of late had an opportunity of conversing upon political topics frequently with his noble friend the noble Duke, he had never once asked him a single question upon the matter, taking it for granted, that their Lordships would be unanimous in their ideas upon the necessity of an Enquiry...The only matter that he had ever met with upon the subject, previous to what he had heard in that House, was a letter printed in the Leyden Gazette, which in terms of great indignation represented the various cruelties practiced by our armies in America, and particularly this last most unheard of instance of barbarity, the execution of Colonel Haynes, without a trial, and under circumstances peculiarly distressing to every humane and considerate mind...As soon as he read it, he declared he put it away, as a matter too shocking to be credited, and under a firm persuasion that the whole relation was a gross calumny, founded on falsehood, and that it would shortly be proved to be such. With regard to what had fallen from the noble Viscount, he was perfectly astonished. He never before heard of the doctrine of hanging up an enemy, who had broken his parole.

He had known, and he spoke correctly and distinctly, because he spoke from what he knew, instances of persons having broken their parole, and its being talked of as an unhandsome thing for a gentleman to do and as a matter disgraceful to those who had been guilty of it; but he had not heard of their having been executed for it. If therefore new principles, and those principles of cruelty were to be introduced into our mode of making war, it was highly necessary they should be clearly defined, that all the world might know what principles we mean to govern our conduct by, in the further progress of the war. His Lordship expatiated on the cruelty of Colonel Haynes's case, and particularly stated his respite, as the exposing him to a lingering death. He complained also of two junior officers dooming him to execution, when a senior officer, Colonel Gould, was on the spot. He declared that he never before knew there was more than one Commander in Chief in America. He asked if it was not worth while to enquire by what power Lord Rawdon disposed of life and death; if he had it from Lord Cornwallis, and Lord Cornwallis from Sir Henry Clinton? Whence did he derive the right of delegating so nice a trust and conveying a power of continuing to delegate it? His Lordship took also a full view of the conduct of the war, censured the whole of management of it; said it had been so misconducted, that the Americans had more power in that country than we had, and took an infinite variety of topics under his description.

THE HOUSE OF LORDS' ENQUIRY INTO THE SURRENDER AT
YORK TOWN (EXCERPTS)
February 8, 1782

The Duke of CHANDOS rose to enquire into the causes of the late very serious calamity of the war, the surrender of my Lord Cornwallis and his army to the united forces of France and America...The question was not a matter of impertinent curiosity, not a question of personal interest or anxiety. He took the matter into his consideration upon a much broader basis. We had lost two armies in one war, a matter not to be paralleled in our history! It was high time, therefore, that some enquiry was instituted. It was due to the Public at large, it was also due to the officers who had held high responsible situations in the execution of the war, to all the Admirals and Generals, who had served in America. Let it not be thought, therefore that he had a personal object in view, or that he was actuated by any invisions motive whatever. He neither expected to find, nor meant to search for criminality in individuals...To clear up all errors, to remove all doubts, and to put an end to surmises and suggestions, which, while human nature was human nature, it was almost impossible for the most candid, the most impartial and the most disinterested, to avoid harbouring and suffering to make some impression on their breasts, he was anxious that their Lordships should resolve to form themselves into a Committee of the whole House, and to proceed fairly and with unprejudiced minds to an Enquiry, to obtain the best evidence they could get at, to examine facts with patience and temper, and to draw such conclusions from the whole of the investigation, as should appear to the Committee to be most consonant with strict justice...The Duke moved

"That this House will on Monday next, resolve itself into a Committee of the whole House to enquire into the causes of the great loss which this nation has sustained by the surrender of the whole army under the command of Lieutenant General Earl Cornwallis at York Town and Gloucester, in the province of Virginia, as prisoners of war to the United States of America."

Lord STURMONT rose...and said...a part of its form struck him as not only highly objectionable and improper for that House to admit upon their Journals, but as unnecessary with regard to the sense, which he conceived the noble Duke meant his motion to convey. What he alluded to were the last words of it, which stated that Lord Cornwallis had surrendered his army prisoners of war to the United States of America.

The Duke of GRAFTON observed,...whether it would not be as well to say "surrendered to the arms of those, *calling themselves* the United States of America.

Lord GOWER...thought it might be as well for the noble Duke to wave those words, which had been objected to, and not to let such a trifle stand in the way of unanimity upon a point of the first magnitude. The great object he conceived was to enquire into the cause of the surrender, and not to dwell upon the parties to whom the surrender was made; and if he was right in this regarding it, surely the words in question were perfectly immaterial.

Lord OSBORNE (the Marquis of Carmarthen) recommended altering the motion by omitting altogether the concluding words, and letting it end with the words "surrendered prisoners of war."

The Duke of RICHMOND said, the words "United States of America" struck him as essentially necessary to the motion.

The Lord CHANCELLOR said...With regard to omitting the words *United States of America*, perhaps the Motion would be more full in its extent without those words, than with them. The Motion as it stood, seemed to exclude the surrender of the fleet to the French, from falling within the scope of the intended Enquiry, a matter which he believed was very far from the intention of the noble Duke, or of the House in general.

Lord ABINGDON...remarked that neither that House nor the other, nor both conjoined, were competent to recognize the independence of the United States of America. The constitution had placed an insuperable bar in the way of such a measure which could not be adopted with a gross violation of the constitution.

The Duke of MANCHESTER...observed that though Lord Cornwallis was in England, he could not be called upon to give any information to the House, because he was at this time a prisoner on his parole. Consequently, that all argument about the presence of the parties were inapplicable.

Lord SHELBURNE said...The Motion, in his opinion, would be compleat without the words that had been excepted to; and indeed it would derive some advantage from their being omitted, inasmuch as the letting the motion stand generally, would make it more extensive; and...would not exclude from the Enquiry that part of the surrender at York, the surrender of the fleet, &c. to the French.

The Duke of CHANDOS said...The noble Viscount had talked of the ensuing campaign. He hoped to God, he did not mean another American campaign. It was a matter of great importance. The nation had already suffered sufficiently by American campaigns, and after what had passed, he could not bring himself to imagine that ministers were mad enough to hazard another.

The Motion was put and carried, *nemine dissentiente.*

HOUSE OF COMMONS DEBATE ON YORKTOWN AND AMERICAN WAR
(EXCERPTS)
February 23, 1782

From *The Morning Post & Daily Advertiser.*

General Conway now entered upon the unannounced enquiry into the mode of conducting the American war. He said he felt himself under peculiar circumstances of distress when he considered the vast importance of the business he had undertaken, and his own poor abilities for so great a talk...The General said, it was not his intention to take a retrospect in the detail of the American war. That it has been unfortunate, we all feel. That it is impracticable, we cannot but foresee. It has been unparalleled for its barbarity. It has been unparalleled for its disasters. Let us not then...wed ourselves to desperation; but before it be too late, let us retreat from that gulph into which we now are blindly rushing. I know it from the best authority. I have my information from almost every officer of consequence who has been on service in America, and returned to this country, that Administration has been in every respect deceived by the representation made to them of the situation of the Continent. We have no friends there; and if we ever had any, our cruelties, our murders, our plunders, our rapes, our abandoned vice of every fort has entirely alienated them...If we have any friends there, as my Lord Cornwallis has described them, they are timid. If we have any foes, (and that we have, let a seven years unfortunate and disgraceful war stamp with sad conviction on our minds) they are inveterate. Who that reflects but an instant upon this melancholy posture of our affairs, can hesitate (unless lost to every feeling that gives a dignity to manhood) to embrace any opportunity consistent with good sense, to put an end to a war the most singularly calamitous, that ever fell upon a people, --. Such an opportunity, I am well informed, has been offered to Administration...Good God! Mr. Speaker - How miserable is our prospect after all this waste of treasure? Must this depopulated country still bewail more precious lives than have been squandered. I speak not of our wealth; amazing as that loss is, it is still but trash compared with all the blood that has been shed on this occasion. Sir, Sir, this blood cries loudly against Ministry. They might have saved it. They have enough to answer for. Let them not aggravate their condemnation. Still they may attone...I am well authorised in saying, that at no great distance from this town, there are persons deputed by Congress with sufficient powers for pacification. I would be glad to known, what hinders our embracing them? Is it the pride of conquest? alas! that we have been long strangers to. Is it the increase of our resources? Let our diminished funds speak. Is it the diminution of our foes? Let our adnumerated enemies bear witness...Sir, with all the conviction in my mind which our situation impresses, of the necessity of a peace, I am free to confess I have my apprehensions of a different opinion prevailing in the breast of Government; and a late change in the Ministry confirms my apprehensions...From this knowledge I dread, that although the men are changed, the Ministers are still the same. But, Sir, the fate of the motion which, without any apology, I shall now submit to the House, will, I trust, dissipate my fears, and convince me that the humane professions of our amiable sovereign, in his speech at the opening of this session, are meant to be carried into execution by his Majesty's Administration. Hereupon the General read his motion, which was to the following purport,- "That this House do resolve on a humble Address to the Throne, to implore his Majesty to be graciously pleased no longer to continue a war found impracticable, for bringing America to obedience by force, and to represent to his majesty the zeal of his faithful Commons to support to the utmost of their power, his majesty's benign wishes for the welfare of his people in the attainment of peace."

Lord CAVENDISH seconded the motion. He said...Does Administration conceive that we become more potent every time we are cast to the ground?...Do they pretend to confront a war which has now a sternness in its aspect (terrible as it has been) which we have never yet experienced. I must conjure the House - I must conjure those in it, who have influence to bethink them of our danger. Is this a time for spleen? - Is this a time for poor spite and idle resentment? - For God's sake let us at last act like men. Let us throw aside that peevishness that has degraded, and, which, if kept, will ruin us. Let us return to our ancient magnanimity, and shew that British spirit is not yet extinct. What is spirit? What is honour? When applied to a nation, its meaning is good sense.

Mr. Secretary ELLIS...said, much, he supposed, was expected from him; but as old a member of that House as he was, he was yet but young in office...the present motion, great as my respect is for the Right Honourable mover of it, militates most powerfully against the disposition, I avow. I see not any of those reasons, which doubtless struck him, as grounds for such his wishes. For my own part, I have ever thought that every wise nation has always entered upon a war for no other purpose than to procure itself a peace. And I have thought too, that this desired end was to be obtained, not by exposing (as the proposed Address would do) the incapacity to support a war, but by evincing a power and a spirit to maintain it. Peace, doubtless, is the most desirable of all objects to a civilized people. But let not our own fondness for that object deprive us of its possession; or (what is worse) give it us upon such conditions as Britons - as men should not accept of. What does this motion go to? A declaration to our enemies, that in fact they are superior to us. Is this patriotism? Is this wisdom? Is it prudence? Is it even cunning? No Sir; it is nothing that bears the semblance of intellect It has not even the spirit of madness. It is abject imbecility! But Gentlemen say, do you mean to bend a people to your government against their will? Why no.- So extravagant a thought never entered into the heads of Administration. We had, and have a numerous body of friends in America, who, by the deep-laid schemes of rebellion, have been unfortunately for us, prevented from acting in that concert that must long since have put an end to the war, if happily such concert had taken place. Many disasters have happened - (disasters which the wisest plans are liable to) which were unfavourable to such a concert...We must, therefore, at the present moment conform us to the circumstances that are present. Though we have lost much, it is but a poor argument that we must lose more...True it is we have a numerous foe to deal with; but is it not equally true that we have had comparatively speaking, more powerful hostility to combat with less potent resources...It is suggested that some negotiation for a peace has been offered by the Americans. If such an offer, or such a negotiation has had any existence before my entrance into office, I confess myself a stranger to it...The American revolters are now in the hands of the French.-- They have been misled by a phantom.-- They have been waked from the possession of luxurious freedom, by the embraces of meagre despotism. There they are held fast. Their armies are cloathed - their armies are fed - their armies are paid with Gallic gold. The war is no longer an American - it is a French war; as such we are now to treat it. Formerly we conjured France in Germany and now (the times require it) we must conquer the same persidious power in America.

Mr. BURKE next rose...Let us give it up. Let us not run blindly to our destruction. If Ministry cannot give us, or which is the same, will not give us a gleam of hope to extricate us from the slough of despondency, why shall we, any longer confide in them? Why shall we thus tamely be led to slaughter.- It was thought necessary to ask our concurrence to enter into the war - and with what decency do they now object to the propriety of consulting us on the subject of pacification. I see a return- ing sense of their duty of late pervading this House. I trust in God that sense will be complete on this occasion, and that we will convince the world that although, thro' our national spirit, we have had the boldness to plunge and persevere in error, we can still shew greater magnanimty in treating from it. In this hope I most earnestly intreat the sanction of the House to the salutary motion offered to their consideration by my Right Honourable Friend.

Mr. ADAMS...said that he must confine himself to plain, unadorned argument, such as was suggested to him by the mere contemplation of the terms of the motion now offered to the House; and upon the first view of these, he was of opinion, two grand objections to embracing them would occur to any man who understood our constitution, and was not wholy inobservant of the common incidents of life. The first was that by an address of the nature proposed, we violated the constitution, by taking the executive part up on us, which ought to be with the utmost care preserved from any intermeddling of this House...Permit me than to suppose the resolution entered into, and that his Majesty consented to the prayer of the address. How do we then stand? The French - the Spaniards, - and the Dutch, may strike us when and where they please in America, and yet we must not by this resolution have the power to return the blows; for how can we discriminate the Americans from their allies....We are hereby to declare that the war is impracticable. What does this declaration amount to, but a confession of our inferiority to our enemies. Good heavens! Mr. Speaker, would any man give me credit to whom I should declare myself a bankrupt?...Sir, this is not conduct for men of sense. It is not conduct for the representatives of a great and free people to adopt. Our constitutional deportment should be, if Ministry are so weak or so wicked as to be incompetent to the management of the national affairs, to address the Throne for the removal of the public servants, in whom we (who are the voice of the people) cannot place our confidence. To attempt any other mode of redress for supposed griev- ances is an infraction on our dearest rights. If the executive branch of government be not kept distinct and entire, there is a farewell to all our freedom. There is a farewell to all our greatness. Ministers are divested of their responsibility the moment we tamper with the privileges of the executive power. And from the public nature of all our disquisition, our enemies would not need the precarious information of a spy. By such a senseless resolution as this, we would be no longer five hundred representatives of the people, we would be five hundred cabinet counsellors. The meanest understanding revolts at the idea of such a solicism in politics; and when I have said so much, I hope I need not add that I am inimical to the motion.

Colonel BARRE...Good God! Sir, the situation of our country is unprecedented; and is this a time, when the nation is verging on absolute ruin, to search for precedents to warrant us in these measures, which may avert that destruction. From what has fallen from the New Secretary of State, I can plainly perceive that the same wretched argument and folly which has hitherto promoted and carried on the accursed war, still influences the conduct of Ministers; he says we have many friends in America, and it would be cruel to abandon them to the merciless hands of the Congress. It is an entire delusion; we have no friends in America; and Ministers have been duped into the idea of the contrary by the misrepresentation and falsehoods told them by Refugees here. From their erroneous misinformation we may chiefly attribute our disasters in America. To contradict their lying reports to Government, we need only refer to Lord Cornwallis's public letters. In them he tells you, he met none of those many Loyalists he was made to believe he should in North Carolina; a province in which he stood most in need of them. In his march throughout almost the whole province he says, he found them inveterate enemies. Does this language denote loyalty? Are these the numerous friends and warm advocates for this country, that Ministers are so mighty tender of deferring?...I have it from very good authority, such as cannot be doubted, that Lord Cornwallis could not, with every persuasion in his power, prevail on even a hundred men to arm themselves in his support. From this account of the disposition of the Americans, must not every man endowed with any degree of reason, see the impracticability of subduing America by force.

Lord NORTH...said he viewed the address in two different lights; the first was that it was meant by it we should withdraw our forces from America.- This he understood, was the construction put on it by some of the gentlemen who supported it; and if so, he thought it a measure highly improper, and big with mischief to the nation. What! would you declare to the French, to Spain, to the Dutch, that you intended relinquishing New York, Charlestown, etc., for the sole purpose that they may render that measure impracticable! for the moment you declare your intention, that moment will they use their utmost endeavours to frustrate it. Besides, the address points out no particular place we are to evacuate; are we to give up Canada, Halifax, St. Augustine and the rest of our possessions in America? As to this, we are left totally in the dark. Ministers ought ever to take care when the Legislature dictates to the executive power the propriety of measures, that their meaning could not be misunderstood; in this case it is the very reverse, Administration is left to judge of an address, which from the general manner in which it is worded, may bear several constructions. If I take it in the second point of view, by way of advice to Ministers, I consider it as quite useless, for I am convinced there is not a servant of the Crown that does not as anxiously wish for peace as any member whatsoever. This they have demonstrated by the frequent commissions they have procured to be sent out for that purpose; and as to what an honourable gentleman says of the duplicity of Ministers in regard to the paper wrote by Sir Grey Cooper instead of in any manner whatever, redounding to my discredit, it is the very strongest, and most convincing proof that can be adduced, that my inclination always led me to peace with America. I must declare, notwithstanding all that Gentlemen, who on every occasion oppose Government, have said to the contrary, that the best method, and likeliest to be attended with advantage to the State would be, whenever they found the principles of Ministers clashed with those of Parliament, to address his Majesty for their removal. I am sure it would be more decent than the method now before the House. It has been observed that it was wrong at this crisis to send out a General, whose military ability, bravery and zeal for his country, is acknowledged by everyone who has the honour of knowing him; and yet these very same Gentlemen who condemn this measure, are the first to complain of the danger New York (a post of such importance to this nation) is in danger of being attacked by the united forces of France and America, if the case is as stated by them, did there ever exist at any time a greater necessity of employing an able gallant officer than at this present, particularly as Sir Henry Clinton has desired to be recalled, and Lord Cornwallis who is second in command, in a situation, at the present moment, not capable of succeeding him, and of course, if Sir Guy Carleton was not to go to America, it must devolve on a foreign General, who is the third in command. Their objection to this appointment is of a piece with their conduct, in opposing every measure adopted by administration.

There appeared a considerable majority against the motion!

HOUSE OF LORDS AND HOUSE OF COMMONS DISCUSSION ON THE LOSS OF YORKTOWN (EXCERPTS)
February 28, 1782

Lord TOWNSEND rose and said, conceiving, as he did, that the aim of the House was to get at the real cause of the calamity in question, and to do substantial justice, without injury to the honour, or imputation on the characters, of the officers concerned, he made no doubt but their Lordships would think it necessary to have all the papers before them, which referred in any way whatever to the subject matter of their intended Enquiry...His aim was solely to ascertain if possible, the cause of one of the greatest national calamities that had ever befallen this or any other country...

The House immediately resolved itself into a Committee, and the Lord CHANCELLOR having just the woolsack, Lord SCARSDALE took his seat at the table as Chairman...

In the HOUSE OF COMMONS, General CONWAY rose and said...He wished to refer to any officer who had been in America; and even asked Ministers, if they had ever any encouragement given to them, or had heard anything to make them suppose that the conquest of America was practicable;...he therefore hoped that no gentleman would that evening be so negligent as to afford an opportunity of losing what was so much the interest, indeed he believed he should be justified in saying, the fate of this country! He concluded with moving in the form of a declaratory resolution of the House, "That after the long and fruitless continuance of the offensive war in America for the purpose of subduing the revolted Colonies by force, it is impracticable, inasmuch as it takes from our exertions some part of that strength which ought to be employed against our European enemies, and is contrary to his Majesty's inclination, expressed in his Speech to both Houses, in which he declared it to be his royal wish to restore peace and tranquility."

Lord ALTHORPE seconded the motion, feeling from the sense of his constituents that peace with America was a very desirable object.

(Three other gentlemen supported the resolution).

Lord NORTH rose...Having said so much with regard to the precedents of prerogative, his Lordship came to that part of his argument which related to the proposition of the address, or resolution...He still confessed, he could not understand it, because it still remained equally questionable, and equally unintelligible. Was it meant, that the forces, in the different parts of America, were to be withdrawn from that continent?- If so, the mode by which they were to effect it, was by no means evident to him. Great obstacles stood in their way, and he felt himself, when he considered the idea, in a dilemma, from which he knew not how to get free. If that however was not the case, what was then to be done? Were the troops to remain there passive and inactive without doing anything? If so, would it answer the purpose of the question before the House, or any way tend to their being employed against our European enemies?

KING SENDS MESSAGE TO HOUSE OF COMMONS, FOLLOWED BY GENERAL CONWAY'S REPLY AND MOTION (EXCERPTS), FOLLOWED BY LORD NORTH'S ARGUMENTS (EXCERPTS)
March 5, 1782

The SPEAKER reported to the House that agreeable to their resolution, their Address having been read to his Majesty, his Majesty had been graciously pleased to return the following answer:
"Gentlemen of the House of Commons,
There are no objects nearer to my heart than the ease, happiness, and prosperity of my people.
You may be assured that, in pursuance to your advice, I shall take such measures as may appear to me to be most conducive in restoration of harmony between Great Britain and the revolted colonies, so essential to the prosperity of both; and that my efforts shall be directed in the most effectual manner against our European enemies, until such peace can be obtained as shall consist with the interests and permanent welfare of my kingdoms."
General Conway then rose....The General said, that no man ever felt a more firm attachment and loyalty for his Sovereign then he did; he wished therefore, on every occasion, to shew all possible respect for the Crown, and that he thought the present was a necessary opportunity for

that House to embrace for the purpose of convincing his Majesty, that his so readily providing a concordance with the wishes of his faithful Commons, was to them a matter of fond joy and satisfaction. For this purpose, he meant to make a motion for the thanks of the House to be voted...There was another matter, which he trusted some person or other would take up, and that was a motion to affirm and confirm the measure adopted last Wednesday. Upon this there might, though he was willing to hope there would not, be some variety of opinion and some argument. Undoubtedly all those who had done him the honour to support his former motion, would do him the same honour now...

Lord ALTHORPE rose and seconded the motion... General CONWAY then rose and said...in all the debates on the subject, not one syllable had been said by Ministers to two very material suggestions thrown out by him, and which appeared to him to be of the first importance. These were, first, That he had good reason to believe, there was at this time in America, a strong propensity, and a sincere inclination, to make peace with the mother country. The second; that there were not far distant from that House, certain persons empowered by Congress to treat for peace. In addition to these, the General said, he had heard that conditions of a new Treaty between France and America were talked of. If therefore an opportunity was to be seised for Great Britain's making a Truce, or agreeing upon a cessation of arms with America, this was in his mind not only the most favourable opportunity, but the most necessary opportunity for proceeding without delay, and in the most effectual manner to come to such an agreement. At present, he was pretty sure there was no bar whatever to impede the effecting a Truce; but in a short time, for the reasons he had stated, the attempt might be impracticable. For these reasons the General said, he moved (what was substantially) the following resolution. "It being the opinion of this House, that the farther prosecution of offensive war on the continent of North America, for the purpose of reducing the revolted Colonies to obedience by force, will be the means of weakening the efforts of this country against her European enemies, tends, under present circumstances, dangerously to increase the mutual enmity so fatal to the interests both of Great Britain and America, and by preventing an happy reconciliation with that country, to frudrate the earnest desire graciously expressed by His Majesty to restore the blessings of public tranquility; and his Majesty having been graciously pleased to declare, that there were no objects nearer his heart, than the ease, happiness and prosperity of his people, and to assure this House, that in pursuance of their advice, he should take such measures, as should appear to him to be most conducive to the restoration of harmony between Great Britain and the revolted Colonies, so essential to the prosperity of both; and that his efforts should be directed in the most effectual manner against our European enemies, until such a peace can be obtained, as shall consist with the interest and permanent welfare of his kingdoms."

Resolved,

"That whoever shall be hereafter concerned in advising, or by any means attempting the further prosecution of offensive war on the continent of North America, for the purpose of reducing the revolted Colonies to obedience by force, are by this House declared enemies of their country, and shall be considered and treated as enemies of their country ought to be treated, &c.&c."

Lord ALTHORPE rose to second this motion...

As soon as the SPEAKER had read the motion, Lord NORTH rose and said, he was glad to find that the first motion had passed, that he should have been extremely sorry had it not passed unanimously; Because undoubtedly it became that House to vote their thanks to his Majesty, for the gracious manner in which he had been pleased to declare his royal intention of complying with the sense of Parliament expressed in their Address of Wednesday last....With regard to the present motion he saw no necessity for it whatever; it was, he conceived, designed to give weight and strength to the Vote of Wednesday, and to make that stronger which in his opinion was strong enough already. It was then, and it ever had been deeply impressed on his mind, that the Minister who should dare to disobey the sense of Parliament, when that sense was solemnly declared was highly culpable, and guilty of a crime of a most heinous nature. Conscious therefore as he was, that as long as he held his present situation, it was at all times his indispensible duty to obey the voice of that House strictly and fully, he could not feel the force of any of those reasons, which had been stated in support of the motion by the Right Hon. Gentleman who moved it, and by the noble Lord who seconded it;...his opinion was still the same and that he thought, when Parliament took upon itself to direct Ministers as to their future conduct in the prosecution of a war, or in the measures to be adopted for the obtainment of peace, it was necessary that their directions should be as explicit, as free from doubt, and a possibility of misconception, as the most precise use of words could render them, for the very reason such he had already declared, viz. because when the sense of Parliament was known ministers stood without excuse, and were certainly highly criminal, if they did not strictly obey those directions which Parliament had thought proper to give. A majority, therefore, having decided against his opinion, he felt himself bound to consider the declaration of that majority as the declaration of Parliament and to obey it implicitly...Were Ministers to understand anything by the present motion, or by that which had been voted on Wednesday last, other than that they were to hold perpetually in their view, that it was the sense of Parliament to make Peace with America, as soon as possible, and to seize the earliest opportunity that might offer for that purpose? Were they to consider themselves as bound to act in this manner; and that, by so doing, they would comply with the voice of that House.--

General CONWAY rose again...The General added some other arguments to prove that the terms he had adopted were perfectly intelligible, that they certainly were not to give Ministers any instructions to seize the first opportunity that might offer of making peace, but immediately to forego any further prosecution of offensive war with America, for the purpose of reducing America to obedience by force.

ENQUIRY BY THE HOUSE OF LORDS INTO THE SURRENDER AT
YORKTOWN (EXCERPTS)
March 7, 1782

The Duke of CHANDOS declared that he had not the smallest intention of drawing any conclusion from the papers then on the table, that
could in the least degree affect the characters of the officers who had
commanded in America. On the contrary, he had moved to have those
papers read, because he was convinced from the evidence of those
papers, that the Commanders in America had done their duty, and
deserved the thanks of their country for their conduct. Nothing could, in
his mind, be more strongly and undeniably substantiated by written
proof, than those papers substantiated the fact that the Cabinet alone
was to blame, and not the Commanders. The Cabinet had clearly
planned unwisely, and supported the executions of their own plans
weakly and inadequately. There was not in possibility a better proof of
any fact to be obtained than the proof on the table, that the Cabinet were
the sole cause of the disaster that had befallen the gallant army under its
brave and noble General, the Earl of Cornwallis. The letters explained
their whole system of conduct, for the Committee could not but have
observed that the King's Ministers had repeatedly ordered expeditions, in
order to be capable of undertaking which, the Commanders had written
for reinforcements, and those reinforcements had been sent them by
dribblets, and never in time for the purposes they were designed to
assist in effecting. But it was not, his Grace said, to any military proceeding that the capture of Lord Cornwallis's army was owing, so much
as to the want of our having a proper naval force in America. To that
fatal neglect of the best and wisest exertions this country could make
was the misfortune to be attributed; and when he said this, he declared
he meant not particularly to point out the first Lord of the Admiralty.
That Officer of the Crown was not individually responsible for the expeditions, planned by the Cabinet...The noble Earl was but one of the many;
and it was the Cabinet, collectively, that he considered as answerable for
the loss of Lord Cornwallis's army. They ought to have seen the necessity of the case, and to have had a stronger naval force on the American
station. Had they done so, they might have prevented the possibility of
such a calamity's befalling us in two ways; they might either have
prevented the French fleet under Monsieur de Grasse from entering the
Chesapeak, or they might have blocked them up after they had entered
it, and by that means have effected the same end...He had no personal
intentions whatever, but meant to make the conduct of the Ministers the
object of his conclusions, said, he designed to move two resolutions: the
one to resolve that the cause of the capture of the army under Lord
Cornwallis was the want of a sufficient naval force to cover and protect
the same; the other, to resolve that the King's Ministers had acted in a
manner highly criminal in having neglected to send a proper naval force
to America for that purpose. His Grace concluded with moving his first
Resolution in the following words: "That it is the opinion of this Committee, that the immediate cause of the capture of the army under Earl
Cornwallis in Virginia, appears to have been the want of a sufficient
naval force to cover and protect the same."

CHAPTER VII

March 9, 1782 - December 1782

From
The Morning Chronicle and London Advertiser
(unless otherwise noted)

(All quotations, except headings)

HOUSE OF COMMONS OFFERS MOTION FOR THE REMOVAL OF
MINISTERS (EXCERPTS)
March 9, 1782

Lord John CAVENDISH rose and said, such was the alarming and
singular situation of the country that he felt himself impelled by every
principle of duty to his constituents, and by every feeling of regard for the
remaining part of the British dominion, to call the attention of the House
to the real state of affairs. His Lordship then went into a consideration of
the expence incurred by the war, observing that gentlemen were so much
in the habit of voting large sums year after year, that probably few of
them gave themselves the trouble of examining into the whole account of
the money expended and the total that it amounted to. He had taken the
pains, and a painful task it was, to look into the amount of the several
votes collectively for the Army, Navy and Ordnance, since the commencement of the war, and Gentlemen probably would be a little astonished to hear that the expence of those articles alone had cost the country, since the commencement of the war, upwards of one hundred millions...He intended to move four resolutions. The first to declare the sum
the war had cost this country in the articles of Army, Navy nd Ordnance
during its continuance; the second, to state our losses as they really
stood; the third, to say that we were at war in Europe with France,
Spain, and Holland, without a single ally; and the fourth to declare it as
the opinion of that House that the calamities and expences incurred as
stated in the three preceding resolutions, were owing to the want of foresight and the want of ability in his Majesty's Ministers.

CONTINUATION OF REMOVAL OF MINISTERS (EXCERPTS)
March 11, 1782

Mr. FOX went on to remind the House that...respecting the necessity
of an immediate change of Administration; he said, the country required

a combination of all the wisdom and all the vigour to be collected in the nation. What had the noble Lord in the blue ribband, expressly told the House on Wednesday fortnight, but that if the sense of the House was against him, he would instantly go to his Sovereign and resign? Why had not the noble Lord kept his word? Did he flatter himself the sense of the House was not against him? A majority had decided against him...What was to be expected from an American Secretary, and a Minister, who severally maintained their former sentiments respecting America, and who considered the vote of Wednesday fortnight, as a setter on their inclinations! The times required it, and he hoped to God, the country would soon have an administration settled on a broad bottom, in which they could place confidence, and from whose measures they might rationally hope for success. It was by driving the present weak, wicked and incapable advisers of the Crown, from about the person of his Majesty, that the country could alone expect to recover from its present disgrace and misfortune. The propositions moved by his noble friend that day, he was convinced in his own mind, would tend to produce that great and desirable effect, which every well-wisher to Great Britain must anxiously long for, and therefore wishing as he did for the removal of the noble Lord in the blue ribband, and such of his colleagues, as had been the planners and conductors of the accursed American war, as the best blessing he could wish for his country.

The Lord ADVOCATE rose...The noble Lord, who had introduced the motion, and all its supporters, had attributed our present unfortunate situation to the want of foresight, and want of ability of Ministers, and had taken up the facts on which they rested that assertion, from the year 1775. He was ready, peremptorily, to deny the assertion in the first place, and next to maintain that all our present misfortunes had their origin in the American war. Indeed, there was scarcely a Gentleman on the other side of the House, at all accustomed to speak on political subjects, who had not at one time or other expressly declared as much: but in order to see how the American War commenced, and to whom its origin was ascribeable, he should contend it was necessary to look a great way farther back than the year 1775. The American War, in his opinion, was to be ascribed to the extraordinary irresolute, weak, and contradictory measures government, and of those Administration, which first passed the American Stamp Act, then repealed it, and then passed the Declaratory Act. That the American war was in its beginning a popular war, and that it was supported by the voice of the nation, was a truth not to be denied. It certainly was so, as certainly as it was at that moment very much disliked, on account of the expence of blood and money it had cost the country, the extensive and complicated war in which it had involved us, and the difficulties and calamities it had drawn down upon us. The French, our natural and insidious foes, had watched the opportunity, the American war gave them of quarreling with Great Britain, in order to resent our having beat them last war, to recover some of their conquered possessions, to diminish our power, to lessen our force, and to tarnish our glory.

A COUNTRY GENTLEMAN'S LETTER PUTTING BLAME OF THE WAR'S
MISFORTUNE ON COMMANDERS (EXCERPTS)
March 29, 1782

Gentlemen and fellow-subjects,

I address you as men under no bias whatever, except that resulting
from convictions. The only public interest you profess or can have, is the
welfare of your country and constitution. I view you as independent
legislators of the British empire, and as individuals possessed with the
power and inclination to render service to the state, but may want, or at
least seems to want, a method of serving your country, or of rightly
understanding her true interest. I will endeavour to draw a line, and if
you will hold to that line, I will be bold to affirm, that Great Britain will
soon soar above all her enemies.

1st. Though no earthly constitution can be perfect, I believe the
British is the best. Endeavour to preserve that happy constitution.

2dly, Though war is highly destructive, yet when you find that your
country is involved in it, try to promote success.

3dly. Pursue the American war, because all rebellions ought to be
suppressed; but then pardon and grant the Americans all the constitutional advantages which an Englishman can enjoy. They can ask no
more, nor can you give more...

Though the present administration are in my opinion by no means
competent for the carrying on the war, by no means remarkable for the
goodness of their intelligence, the wisdom of their plan, or the execution
of their measures, yet I am afraid to wish them turned out, or their
places filled by other men of the Minority, because I suspect that the
principles which those men discover and avow, are too precipitate and
narrow to restore this country to her former glory and greatness. That it
may yet be done, I boldly affirm, and that even if the plans of Ministry,
imperfect as they were, were but duly executed, the most signal success
must have marked almost every step that was taken. Hence I conclude,
the Commanders are to blame, and from those conclusions, observe the
essentials necessary for insuring a successful war in future, are to make
public examples of some of those great Commanders, and to convince all
others, that no attention will be paid to any other consideration than
pure merit, to be judicious and indefatigable in procuring the earliest
and best intelligence, and to avail the state, by counteracting the designs
of the enemy in every quarter, and making impressions upon them every
time that there is an opportunity of doing so...

I conceive that the principle and the abilities of Lord Shelburn, if in
office, would restore this country, guide a successful war, and in due
time obtain a firm adequate, and lasting Peace. I wish that great man
was in office, he would bring the Americans to a sense of their duty and
allegiance, and he would preserve to them their rights as subjects; what
can they wish more? What more can England give?

Lord Shelburn come into office, your country calls you! Ministers
admit him, or turn out and make room for him. We want the grandeur of
our country restored, before it be too late, and he only can do it!

LETTERS OF SIR GUY CARLETON, GENERAL WASHINGTON AND REPLY FROM CONGRESS (EXCERPTS)
July 13, 1782

Headquarters, New York, May 7, 1782.

Having been appointed by his Majesty to the command of the forces on the Atlantic Ocean, adjoined with Admiral Digby in the commission of Peace, I find it proper in this manner to apprise your Excellency of my arrival at New York...

I am much concerned to find that private and unauthorised persons have on both sides given way to those passions which ought to have received the strongest and most effectual control, and which have begot acts of retaliation, which, without proper prevention, may have an extent equally calamitous and dishonourable to both parties, though as it should seem more extensively pernicious to the natives and settlers of this country.

I am further to acquaint you, Sir, that it was my intention to have sent this day a similar letter of compliment to Congress, but am informed it is previously necessary to obtain a passport from your Excellency, which I therefore hope to receive, if you have no objection for the passage of Mr. Morgan to Philadelphia.

Guy Carleton

Headquarters, May 10, 1782.

Ever since the commencement of this unnatural war, my conduct has borne invariable testimony against those inhuman excesses, which in too many instances have marked its various progress.

With respect to a late transaction, to which I presume your Excellency alludes, I have already expressed my fixed resolution, a resolution formed on the most mature deliberation, and from which I shall not recede.

I have to inform your Excellency, that your request of a passport for Mr. Morgan to go to Philadelphia will be conveyed to Congress by the earliest opportunity, and you may rest assured that I will embrace the first moment to communicate to you their determination thereon.

Many inconveniences and disorders having arisen from an improper admission of flags at various posts of the two armies, which have given rise to complaints on both sides - to prevent abuses in future, and for the convenience of communication, I have concluded to receive all flags from within your lines at the Post of Dobb's Ferry, and nowhere else, so long as the headquarters of the two armies remain as at present.

G. Washington

By the United States in Congress, assembled May 14, 1782.

The letter of the 10th, from the Commander in Chief, being read, inclosing a copy of a letter to him from Sir Guy Carleton, dated head quarters, New York, May 2, 1782.

Resolved, That the Commander in Chief be and hereby is directed to refuse the request of Sir Guy Carleton, of a passport for Mr. Morgan to bring dispatches to Philadelphia.

Published by order of the Congress.

FINANCES OF THE AMERICAN STATES
July 15, 1782

The Paper established by the British Government in America, had a real credit, and was even preferred to silver and gold in common circulation. The paper which has been substituted both by the particular states, and by the Congress, lost its value, even in the first months of their enthusiasm; but some time since it is fallen into *the utmost discredit*, so that a ducat of gold, is actually worth 18 ducats in paper. The want of economy, the malversations exercised in all the departments, the monopolies which they have sought in vain to repress, by laws which it was necessary every year to revoke, that avidity of which the most considerable persons set an example, have obliged the Congress to circulate a prodigious quantity of this money, and of consequence to render it of no value in the public opinion. The operations of finance, announced last year, *could not establish confidence* - for those who were the most zealous for independence, feared with justice, lest the intestine wars, which would inevitably arise, should hinder the promised liquidation of the part of Congress. This paper has been the nerve of war, but at present, interest is the most powerful of all motives, especially with the Americans, this paper may become the bond which will re-unite the States of America, with the mother country.

It is equally embarrassing in the present conjecture, to give or to refuse money to the Americans. If you refuse it them, they will murmur, and will be incapable of sustaining their independence. If you grant it them it cannot be dissembled, that the taxes which the English sought to impose on them were only the pretext and apparent cause of the war, but that the danger of a general bankruptcy on their part has been one of its principal causes.

THE KING MAKES NEW APPOINTMENTS
July 15, 1782

At the Court at St. James's, the 10th of July, 1782.
PRESENT
The KING'S Most Excellent Majesty in Council.

This day the Right Honourable William Pitt, Chancellor and Under Treasurer of His Majesty's Exchequer, was, by his Majesty's command sworn of his Majesty's Most Honourable Privy Council, and took his place at the board accordingly.

His Majesty having been pleased to appoint the Right Honourable Thomas Townshend, to be one of his Majesty's Principal Secretaries of State, he was this day, by his Majesty's command, sworn one of his Majesty's Principal Secretaries of State accordingly.

Whitehall, July 13.

The King has been pleased to constitute and appoint the Right Honourable William Earl of Shelburne of the kingdom of Ireland, Knight of the most noble Order of the Garter, the Right Honourable William Pitt, James Grenville, Richard Jackson, and Edward James Elliot, Esquires, to be Commissioners for executing the Office of Treasurer of his Majesty's Exchequer.

The King has been pleased to constitute and appoint the Right Honourable Augustus Viscount Keppel, Sir Robert Harland, Bart. Admiral Hugh Pigot, Charles Brett, Richard Hopkins, John Jefferies Pratt, and John Aubrey, Esqrs. to be his Majesty's Commissioners for executing the Office of Lord High Admiral of the Kingdoms of Great Britain and Ireland, and of the dominions, islands, and territories thereunto respectively belonging.

The King has been pleased to constitute and appoint the Right Honourable Sir George Yonge Bart, to his Majesty's Secretary at War.

CAPITULATION OF THE BAHAMA ISLANDS, ARTICLE I ONLY
July 15, 1782

Articles of Capitulation agreed on at Nassau in New Providence, this 8th day of May 1782...

Article I. THE possession of the Islands of New Providence, Eleuthers, and Harbour Island, as also of all other the Bahama Islands, together with the artillery, powder, arms, ammunition, and stores, as also all the forts and posts in the same, now in possession of the troops of his Britanic Majesty, shall be delivered up to the troops of his Catholic Majesty, together with an inventory thereof.

A HUMOROUS SPY STORY
July 18, 1782

An evening paper says, the following particulars of a plan for seizing General Greene, and dispensing, if not debauching his whole army is authentic.

Some short time ago, a man ran away with a horse belonging to an Officer in General Green's army, and got to Charlestown; the General sent a flag to the Commanding Officer of that garrison, to demand the man and horse; the answer returned to him was, that it was impossible to give up the man, as he had put himself under the King's protection, but that the owner of the horse should have his property on sending for it. When this answer was carried back to General Greene's camp, the Officer sent his Sergeant, whose name was Peters, to Charles Town, to bring back the horse. While the Sergeant was in the town, he was sounded as to his attachment to the cause in which he was embarked, and his fidelity to his Commander, and it was found that he loved money much better than either his Commander or his cause. As soon as this discovery was made, it was proposed to him that he should sound the Sergeants of the Rebel army, and see if they could be gained over, to deliver up their General, and receive the English into their camp. Large offers of money were made; and as an earnest of what he might expect, if he should succeed, a very considerable sum was given to him upon the spot. Peters, though faithless to his cause and his Commander, was true to the promises he had made at Charles Town. - He sounded almost the whole corps of Sergeants, and found them disposed just as he could have wished.- The plot was well laid, and Peters used to go frequently with a flag to Charles Town, upon business entrusted to him by his own Officers. - At his last journey to that town, he had a long conference with our people, and then it was agreed, that on a particular day, which he named, a party of British Lighthorse, to consist of 250 men, should at a certain hour be drawn up near the strip of a wood, which flanked Greene's camp; and there they were to remain till he should make a particular signal; this signal was to be made without fail, at a fixed time, if everything was ready in the camp for the execution of the design.

This well concerted scheme was overturned by - female curiosity. The wife of one of the Sergeants was surprised at the frequent visits he used to make at night (to meet the conspirators) and suspecting that there was an intrigue in question, she resolved to discover, if possible, who was her rival. She followed her husband in the dark, till she came to the tent where the Sergeants met, and listening carefully, she heard sufficient to convince her, that love was not the object that had made her husband go out; and though she was not able to discover the particulars of the affair, she nevertheless heard enough to be assured that a conspiracy of some kind was afoot; she immediately went to General Greene's tent, and after having stipulated for a pardon for her husband, discovered all she knew; - the conspirators were seized, and examined separately, but Peters was the only one among them who was fully acquainted with every particular; and he refused to make any discovery for some time. The reason for delaying it was generous on his part; it was then night, and the attempt was to be made at day break; he knew, therefore, that by agreement, the English horse must have been at that time lying in the place, which he had pointed out as the fittest for the ambuscade; and he knew also, that if he was to disclose all the particulars of the conspiracy at that time, this party must be either cut to pieces or taken prisoners; The light-horse were in fact at the appointed place to their time, and having waited beyond the appointed hour for the expected signal and not seeing it, they concluded that all was not right, and therefore they rode back to Charles Town. This was what Peters expected; and in the morning he made a full discovery of the plan, but without naming his accomplices. The consequence was, that he was immediately hanged, with others of the conspirators who were apprehended with him; and General Greene, when the Gentleman from whom we received the above particulars left Charles Town, was taking every measure to discover to what extent the contagion of defection had spread itself in his army.

COMMUNICATION BETWEEN CLINTON, ROBERTSON AND GENERAL WASHINGTON, RE: EXECUTION OF CAPTAIN HUDDY (EXCERPTS)
July 23, 1782

Headquarters, April 21, 1782.
...To save the innocent, I demand the guilty. Captain Lippincott, therefore, or the Officer who commanded at the execution of Captain Huddy, must be given up; or if that officer was of inferior rank to him, so many of the perpetrators, as will, according to the tariff of exchange, be an equivalent.

95

To do this, will mark the justice of your Excellency's character; in failure of it, I shall hold myself justifiable in the eyes of God and Man, for the measure to which I shall resort.

I beg your Excellency to be persuaded, that it cannot be more disagreeable to you to be addressed in this language, than it is to me to offer it; but the subject requires frankness and decision.

I have to request your speedy determination, as my resolution is suspended but for your answer

George Washington

New York, April 25, 1782.

...And though I am extremely concerned for the cause, I cannot conceal my surprise and displeasure at the very improper language you have use of, when you could not but be sensible was totally unnecessary.

The mildness of the British Government does not admit of acts of cruelty, or persecuting violence, and as they are notoriously contrary to the tenor of my own conduct and disposition, (having never yet stained my hands with innocent blood), I must claim the justice of having it believed, that if such have been committed by any persons under my command, they could not have been warranted by my authority, nor can they ever have the sanction of my approbation. My personal feelings, therefore required no such incitements to urge me to take every proper notice of the barbarous outrage against humanity, which you have represented to me, the moment it came to my knowledge. And accordingly, when I heard of Captain Huddy's death, (which was only four days before I received your letter,) I instantly ordered a strict enquiry to be made into all its circumstances, and shall bring the perpetrators of it to an immediate trial. To sacrifice innocence, under the notion of preventing guilt, in place of suppressing, would be adopting barbarity, and raising it to the greatest height. Whereas, if the violators of the laws of war, are punished by the Generals, under whose powers they act, the horrors which those laws were formed to prevent, will be avoided, and every degree of humanity, war is capable of, maintained.

Could violations of humanity be justified by examples, many, from the parts where your power prevails, that exceed, and probably gave rise to this in question, could be produced. In hope that the mode I mean to pursue, will be adopted by you, and prevent all future enormities.

H. Clinton

New York, May 1, 1782.

...A court-martial is appointed to try the person complained of, and all his abetters in the death of Huddy, by Sir Henry Clinton, who had taken measures for this, before he received any letter from you on the subject.

James Robertson

Head Quarters, May 5, 1782.

...Your Excellency is acquainted with the determination expressed in my letter of the 21st of April to Sir Henry Clinton. I have now to inform you, that so far from receding from that resolution, orders are given to designate a British officer for retaliation. The time and place are fixed.

But I still hope, the result of your Court Martial will prevent this dreadful alternative.

Sincerely lamenting the cruel necessity, which alone can induce so distressing a measure; in the present instance, I do assure your Excellency, I am as earnestly desirous as you can be, that the war may be carried on, agreeable to the rules which humanity formed, and the example of the politest nations recommends, and shall be extremely happy in agreeing with you, to prevent or punish every breach of the rules of war, within the spheres of our respective commands...

George Washington

BOARD OF LOYALISTS REPORTS: CAPTAIN HUDDY'S EXECUTION A NECESSITY (EXCERPTS)
(Included in the letter to Sir Henry Clinton, dated April 27)
July 29, 1782

In compliance with the orders of the honourable Board of Direction, we beg leave to communicate to your Excellency, for their information, an account of the proceedings of the Loyalists from Monmouth, on the late expedition for the relief of Captain Clayton Tilton, and two other Loyalists, then prisoners with the rebels in that country.

Being frustrated in design off Capt. Tilton, by force, and *our offers for exchange rejected*, we dreaded that he was reserved for a fate similar to that our associate Philip White had suffered, who was taken at the same time with Captain Tilton, and inhumanly and wantonly murdered by the guard who were carrying him to Monmouth gaol.

This recent instance of cruelty, added to the many daring acts of the same nature which have been perpetrated with impunity, by a set of vindictive rebels, well known by the name of *Monmouth Retaliators*, associated and headed by one General Furman, who horrid acts of cruelty have gained him universally the name of *Black David*, fired our party with an indignation only to be felt by men who for a series of years have beheld, many of their friends and neighbours butchered in cold blood, under the usurped form of law, and often without that ceremony, for no other crime than that of maintaining their allegiance to the government under which they were born, and which the rebels audaciously call treason against their states.

We thought it high time to convince the rebels, we would no longer tamely submit to such glaring acts of barbarity, and though we lament the necessity to which we have been driven, to begin a retaliation of intolerable cruelties, long continued, and often repeated, yet we are convinced that we could not have saved the life of Captain Tilton, by any other means. We therefore pitched upon Joshua Huddy, for a proper subject for retaliation, because he was not only well known to have been a very active and cruel persecutor of our friends, but had not been ashamed to boast of his having been instrumental in hanging Stephen Edwards, a worthy loyalist, and the first of our brethren who fell a martyr to republican fury in Monmouth county. Huddy was the man who tied the knot, and put the rope about the neck of that inoffensive sufferer. This fact will appear by two affidavits, which we have the honour to enclose. When the board are pleased to take into their consideration the motives which induced us to take this step, and that Huddy was executed in the county where so many acts of cruelty must have been committed on Refugees, we hope they will not think our conduct reprehensible...

A LETTER FROM CHARLESTOWN, RELATING THE STORY OF
SAVANNAH (EXTRACTS)
August 26, 1782

Dated July 8, 1782.
But the present scene of evacuation of Savannah is nearest our country and nearest our pitying hearts. What will the generous Briton say, when he hears so many loyal subjects are obliged to leave all his real, and some of his personal property in a province declared to be in the King's Peace? And leave their fields loaded with rice and corn, just ripening for harvest?...As St. Augustine is not to be evacuated, many planters from Savannah will go to East Florida with their negroes; their cattle, etc. must be abandoned as well as their fields to the enemy; several gentlemen have applied to General Leslie for leave to carry their slaves to the number of 2,000 to Jamaica, which was readily granted, and every indulgence which such unmerited difficulty and distress could desire relief under. What will be the fate of this town, God knows. When I consider the very expensive and strong fortifications, the great number of Loyal Refugees within them, and the immense value of British goods in this town, I cannot think it will be evacuated by order, and it must be a force superior to any in these parts to take it; the common report through the country is, that it will soon be evacuated, and it is needless to take it by force. The sale of confiscated estates go on as quietly as if it was in the midst of England. Negroes, I mean able workers, were lately sold at three and five guineas a head, such as seven years ago would average above 70 sterling each, nay old and young...
When the report of evacuating St. Augustine, where there are so many refugees from this country, retired with the wreck of their fortune, they were almost in a rage and declared they would not leave the province of East Florida, although the King's troops were drawn off; they declared, that rather than be taken by, or submit to Congress, they would invite the Spaniards to take possession of his old Castle, in case Great Britain abandoned its loyal subjects there; and this, I believe they would certainly have done.

A POEM ON BENJAMIN FRANKLIN'S INVENTIONS
September 9, 1782

The following lines by an Episcopal Clergyman of Brunswick, N.J., I believe never yet have made their way to the public, by giving them a place in your agreeable paper, you will oblige.
J.H.M.

Inscription on a curious Chamber Stove, in the form of an Urn, contrived
in such a manner as to make the flame descend, instead of ascending
from the fire. Invented by Dr. Franklin.

Like a Newton sublimely he soared
   To a summit before unattained
New regions of science explored
   And the palm of Philosophy gained.

With a spark that he caught from the skies
   He displayed an unparalled wonder
And we saw with delight and surprize
   That his rod could save us from thunder.

O! Had he been wise to pursue
   The track for his talents design'd
What a tribute of praise had been duer
   To the father and friend of mankind.

But to covet political fame,
   Was in him a degrading ambition;
A spark that from Lucifer came
   And kindled the blaze of sedition.

Let candour then write on his urn,
   Here lies the renown'd inventor
Whose flame to the skies ought to burn
   But inverted, descends to the center.

A PROBLEM WITH FRENCH-AMERICAN ALLIANCE
September 21, 1782

A very considerable part of the people of America are much alarmed
by the apprehension that the ultimate design of their great and good ally,
is to subjugate the whole continent to the intolerable yoke of religious
and civil tyranny and therefore severely regret that they did not longer
persevere in their endeavors to obtain a redress of grievances by argument and expostulation, instead of rashly resolving, in the moment of
passion and resentment, to emancipate themselves from the mild authority of the British Legislature. The revolt of New York from the Congress,
seems to forebode, that the other provinces will be soon convinced, that
the pretended friendship of the House of Bourbon had its origin in the
insidious design of robbing them of that freedom of which both France
and Spain have, with the cunning and plausibility characteristic of both
nations, affected to be so disinterestedly solicitous of securing to them a
permanent possession.

A private letter from Paris says, that the Compte de Rochambeau is
ordered home from America, on account of some disagreement between
him and the Americans; the French being willing at this time to do everything in their power to oblige them, that they may not compromise
matters with England.

99

A POEM SAYING THAT THE CONQUEST OF AMERICA BY FIRE AND SWORD IS NOT TO BE ACCOMPLISHED
October 2, 1782

Written on a late Declaration of Lord C---'s
        True is the Patriotic word,
    We never can by fire and sword,
    The fierce American subdue;
    If we our General's steps pursue,
    His own allies, who tears and rends,
    And turns his sword against his friends.

    The loyal, if he first invite,
    For Britain, and its King to fight,
    Promise to succour and protect,
    He then abandons to neglect;
    Or draws them in an easy prey,
    For their inveterate foes to stay.

    Poor credulous slaves, if he allure,
    By flatt'ring hopes of refuge sure,
    Their cruel tyrants to desert;
    He then with an unfeeling heart,
    Leaves them, who on his faith rely
    By hunger, or desease to die.

    Thousands, who unconsum'd remain,
    He drives out of his camp again,
    (While trusting in his treacherous word)
    Gives up the victims to their lords,
    To punish in the lingering fire,
    By varied torments to expire.

    Such faithful leaders we allow,
    Pit to succeed immortal H-e;
    Who fierce Americans subdu'd,
    And conquer'd them when e'er he would;
    Too generous to pursue his blow,
    Or rample on a vanquish'd foe.

    His vanquish'd foe full oft, he rear'd,
    And kindly their despondences cheer'd
    Too brave to take them by surprize;
    He saw their straits with pitying eyes;
    And put them out of all their pain,
    And gave them back their towns again.

    Such Gen'rals never can aspire,
    Rebels to quell with sword or fire;
    But without fire, another can
    Accomplish it - an honest man,

Who truth and public faith approves,
And more than life his country loves,

A man for this great end design'd,
Our nation now expects to find,
By providential love bestow's
Whose object is Britannia's good;
Britannia's peace his only aim,
And Carleton is the Patriot's name.

UNITED STATES WILL NOT MAKE A SEPARATE PEACE AGREEMENT WITH GREAT BRITAIN WITHOUT THEIR ALLIES (EXCERPTS)
November 19, 1782

From *The Freeman's Journal* of October 5.
By the United States in Congress assembled,
October 4, 1782.

Whereas by the Articles of Confederation and perpetual Union, the sole and exclusive right of making peace is invested in the United States in Congress assembled; and by the treaty of alliance between his Most Christian Majesty and these United States, it is declared, that neither of the contracting parties shall conclude peace nor truce with Great Britain, without the consent of the other; and the Ministers Plenipotentiaries of these United States in Europe, are invested with full power and authority, in their behalf, and in concert with their allies, to negotiate and conclude a general peace; nevertheless it appears the British Court still flatters itself with the vain hope of prevailing on the United States to agree to some terms of dependence upon Great Britain, at least to a separate peace; and there is reason to believe, that Commissioners may be sent to America to offer propositions of that nature to the United States, or that secret emissaries may be employed to delude and deceive. In order to extinguish ill-founded hopes, to frustrate insidious attempts, and to manifest to the whole world the purity of the intentions, and the fixed and unalterable determination of the United States.

Resolved unanimously, That Congress are sincerely desirous of an honourable and permanent peace; that as the only means of obtaining it, they will inviolably adhere to the treaty of alliance with his Most Christian Majesty, and conclude neither a separate peace nor truce with Great Britain; that they will prosecute the war with vigour, until by the blessing of God on the United arms, a peace shall be happily accomplished by which, the full and absolute sovereignty and independence of these United States having been duly assured, their rights as well as those of their allies, shall be effectually provided for and secured.

The Congress will not enter the discussion of any overtures for pacification, but in confidence and in concert with his Most Christian Majesty.

That to guard against the secret artifices and machinations of the enemy, it be, and hereby is recommended to the respective States, to be vigilant and active in detecting and seizing all British emissaries and spies, that they may be brought to condign punishment; that it be enjoined on all officers of departments, charged with persons coming from

101

the enemy, under the protection of flags of truce, to take special care that such persons do not abuse their privileges but be restrained from all intercourse with the country and inhabitants, which is not necessary for transacting the public business on which they may be sent. And lastly, it is recommended to the several States, that no subjects of his Britannic Majesty, coming directly or indirectly from any part of the British dominions, be admitted into any of the United States during the war.

Ordered, That the Honourable the Minister Plenipotentiary of France be furnished with a copy of the above act, and that copies be transmitted to the Ministers of these States at Foreign Courts, and that it be published.

Charles Thompson, Sec.

KING'S PEACE OFFERING IN THE HOUSE OF LORDS, (EXCERPTS)
FOLLOWED BY SOME REPLIES (EXCERPTS)
December 6, 1782

My Lords and Gentlemen,
Since the close of the last Sessions, I have employed my whole time in the care and attention which the important and critical conjuncture of publick affairs required of by me.

I lost no time in giving the necessary orders to prohibit the further prosecution of offensive war upon the Continent of North America. Adopting, as my inclination will always lead me to do, with decision and effect, whatever I collect to be the sense of my Parliament and my People; I have pointed all my views and measures, as well in Europe as in North America, to an entire and cordial reconcilliation with those Colonies.

Finding it indispensible to the attainment of this object, I did not hesitate to go the full length of the powers vested in me, and offered to declare them Free and Independent States, by an article to be inserted in the treaty of peace. Provisional articles are agreed upon, to take effect whenever terms of peace shall be finally settled with the Court of France.

In thus admitting their separation from the Crown of these Kingdoms, I have sacrificed every consideration of my own, to the wishes and opinion of my people. I make it my humble and earnest prayer to Almighty God, that Great Britain may not feel the evils which might result from so great a dismemberment of the empire; and, that America may be free from those calamities, which have formerly proved in the Mother Country how essential monarchy is to the enjoyment of constitutional liberty. Religion, language, interest, affections may, and I hope will yet prove a bond of permanent union between the two countries; To this end, neither attention nor disposition shall be wanting on my part.

While I have carefully abstained from all offensive operations against America, I have directed my whole force by land and sea against the other powers at war, with as much vigour, as the situation of that force, at the commencement of the campaign, would permit...

I have the satisfaction to acquaint you that negotiations to this effect are considerably advanced, the result of which, as soon as they are brought to a conclusion, shall be immediately communicated to you...

I have ordered enquiry to be made into the application of the sum voted in support of the American sufferers; and I trust that you will agree with me, that a due and generous attention ought to be shewn to those, who have relinquished their properties or professions from motives of loyalty to me, or attachment to the Mother Country...

I must recommend to you an immediate attention to the great object of the Public Receipts and Expenditure; and above all, to the State of the Public Debt.- Notwithstanding the great increase of it during the War, it is to be hoped that such regulations may still be established - such savings made - and future loans so conducted, as to promote the means of its gradual redemption by a fixed course of payment.-- I must, with particular earnestness, distinguish for your serious consideration, that part of the debt, which consists of Navy, Ordnance, and Victualling Bills: the enormous discount upon some of these bills, shews this mode of payment to be a most ruinous expedient...

It is the fixed object of my heart to make the general good, and the true spirit of the constitution, the invariable rule of my conduct, and on all occasions to advance and reward merit in every profession...

The Marquis of CARMARTHEN rose up to move for an Address to his Majesty on that occasion. He expressed an hope that the House would be unanimous in testifying their humble gratitude to the Crown for intentions so gracious, for sentiments so paternal, for sacrifices so generous. He declared a full confidence in his Majesty's servants, and that while their conduct should continue to deserve it; they should meet with his support. He was happy, he said, in every opportunity of testifying his respect for the Crown, and doubly happy, when he could testify this respect, on an occasion so happy as the present; when it appeared that the relief, the happiness of his subjects, formed the first wish in the Royal breast. He hoped that peace would soon return to bless the land...The success of his Majesty's arms both by sea and land, during this last campaign, afforded ground to hope that his Ministers would be able to make peace on conditions, fair, safe and honourable. America, he hoped would not yet be wholly lost to Great Britain...

The Earl of SHELBURNE...Maintained that unconditional Independence had not been granted to the Americans; that the *offer* that had been made was not irrevocable; and referred the noble Lord to the words of the Address, which he repeated with emphasis, insisting, that if fair, honourable, and equal terms could not be obtained from France, the ally of America, then the offer (a word on which he laid great stress) might be withdrawn and would cease and determine.

Mr. FOX...Though the Provisional Treaty did not actually put us at peace with America, Mr. Fox said, he conceived it put us in a state so like peace, that we might now consider ourselves as at war but with three enemies, and therefore we should be the better enabled to direct all our efforts against the House of Bourbon. He descanted on the benefits of such a situation, and then went into a consideration of the propriety of making peace. He said a peace was worth obtaining, if only for so short a space as two years; and for these reasons we might in that case be assured we never should have the same four powers combined against us, and we should have leisure to make alliances; he understood there were Courts inclined to assist this country, now we were come to our senses, though they would not join as when we were mad.

Lord NORTH...In the moment, however, that a speedy peace was, and must be the general wish of that House, he begged leave to remind them that we were in a state of actual war, and that every proceeding in Parliament, however directed towards the furtherance of a treaty of pacification, ought to be grounded on the circumstance of our being yet at war, since the only probable means of bringing that war to a safe, a happy, and an honourable issue, was to assure his Majesty, and by that assurance to convince the world, that the Parliament of Great Britain were determined to stand by their Sovereign, and support him at all hazards sooner than accede to any terms of pacification, that were in the least degree disgraceful or dishonourable. With regard to the provisional articles, that had been agreed upon with America, his Lordship said, the matter did not appear to him altogether in the same point of view, in which it was evident, it had struck others. It put us not into any precise situation, either of war or peace, which to him was neither very agreeable, nor very auspicious.

CHAPTER VIII

January - September 1783

From
The Morning Chronicle and London Advertiser
(unless otherwise noted)

(All quotations, except headings)

ARE HOSTILITIES SUSPENDED?
LETTERS FROM GENERAL WASHINGTON TO SIR GUY CARLETON, AND
REPLY (EXTRACTS)
January 14, 1783

From His Excellency General Washington to Sir Guy Carleton, dated Headquarters, September 8, 1782.
I cannot help remarking, that your Excellency has several times lately taken occasion to mention that all hostilities stand suspended on your part. I must confess, that to me this expression wants explanation; I can have no conception of a suspension of hostilities, but that which arises from a mutual agreement of the powers of war, and which extends to naval as well as land operations. That your Excellency has thought proper, on your part, to make a partial suspension, may be admitted; But whether this has been owing to political or other motives is not for me to decide; it is, however, a well known fact, that at the same time the British cruizers on our coast have been more than usually alert; and while Americans are admitted to understand their real interest, it will be difficult for them, when a suspension of hostilities is spoken of, to separate the idea of its extending to sea as well as land.
I cannot ascribe the inroads of savages upon our north-western frontiers to the causes from whence your Excellency supposes them to originate; neither can I allow that they are committed without directions from the Commander in Chief in Canada; for by prisoners and deserters it is apparent, that those ravaging parties are composed of white troops under the command of officers regularly commissioned, as well as savages; and it would be a solecism to suppose, that such parties could be out without the knowledge of their Commander in Chief.

From Sir Guy Carleton to His Excellency General Washington, dated New York, September 12, 1782.
Partial though our suspension of hostilities may be called, I thought

it sufficient to have prevented those cruelties in the Jersies (avowed) which I have had occasion to mention more than once. But if war was the choice, I never expected this suspension should operate further than to induce them to carry it on as is practised by men of liberal minds. I am clearly of opinion with your Excellency, that mutual agreement is necessary for a suspension of hostilities; and that without this mutual agreement, either party is free to act as each may judge expedient; yet I must at the same time frankly declare to you, that being no longer able to discern the object we contend for, I disapprove of all hostilities, both by land and sea, as they only tend to multiply the miseries of individuals, when the public can reap no advantage by success.

As to the savages, I have the best assurances, that from a certain period not very long after my arrival here, no parties of Indians were sent out, and that messengers were dispatched to recall those who had gone forth before that time; and I have particular assurances of disapprobation of all that happened to the party on the side of Sondusky, except so far as was necessary for self-defence.

AGREEMENT ON EXCHANGE OF WAR PRISONERS
January 24, 1783

Charlestown, Oct. 29. The following papers, respecting an exchange of prisoners, are published by authority.
Articles of agreement for the relief and exchange of the prisoners of war, taken in the Southern Department, acceded to, at Accabee, on the 23rd of October, 1782, by Major Wemyss, Deputy Adjutant General, on the part of the Hon. Lieutenant General Leslie, and Major Burnet, on the part of the Hon. Major General Greene.
1st. That all non-commissioned officers and privates, who have been delivered previous to the date hereof, be considered as exchanged, and properly accounted for.
2nd. That all the British prisoners of war, now with the American army, including those lately at George-Town, be sent to Charles-Town, as early as possible, and be considered as exchanged.
3rd. That an immediate exchange of regular Officers, as far as similar rank will apply, shall be effected, and the paroles of the unexchanged Officers to be extended agreeably to their wishes.
4th. That all militia and citizens, both American and British, taken as prisoners of war by either army in the southern department, previous to the date of this agreement, be considered as hereby exchanged; and those who may now be in confinement be immediately liberated.

TRANSLATION OF PRELIMINARIES OF PEACE READ IN HOUSE OF COMMONS
January 28, 1783

Yesterday Mr. Secretary Townsend brought up from the bar a translation of the Preliminaries of Peace between Great Britain and France, signed at Versailles the 20th instant; a Translation of the Preliminaries of Peace between Great Britain and Spain, signed at Versailles the 20th instant; and a copy of the Provisional Treaty with the United States of America, signed the 30th of November last, and the originals of the Preliminaries with France and Spain.

PRELIMINARY ARTICLES AGREED UPON BETWEEN THE UNITED STATES AND GREAT BRITAIN, LISTING ONLY ARTICLES I AND VII (EXCERPTS)
January 30, 1783

ARTICLES *agreed upon, by and between* RICHARD OSWALD, *Esq; the Commissioner of* HIS BRITANIC MAJESTY, *for treating of Peace with the Commissioners of the* UNITED STATES OF AMERICA, *in behalf of His said Majesty, on the one part; and* JOHN ADAMS, BENJAMIN FRANKLIN, JOHN JAY, *and* HENRY LAURENS, *Four of the Commissioners of the said States, for treating of Peace with the Commissioner of His said Majesty, on their behalf, on the other part;*
To be inserted in, and to constitute the Treaty of Peace, proposed to be concluded between the Crown of Great Britain and the said United States; but which Treaty is not to be concluded until Terms of a Peace shall be agreed upon between Great Britain and France, and His Britannic Majesty shall be ready to conclude such Treaty accordingly.
ART. I His Britannic Majesty acknowledges the said United States, viz. New Hampshire, Massachusets Bay, Rhode Island, and Providence Plantations, Connecticut, New York, New Jersey, Pensylvania, Delaware, Maryland, Virginia, North Carolina, South Carolina, and Georgia, to be free, sovereign, and Independent States; that he treats with them as such; and for himself, his heirs and successors, relinquishes all claim to the government, propriety and territorial rights of the same, and every part thereof;...
VII. There shall be a firm and perpetual peace between his Britannic Majesty and the said States, and between the subjects of the one and the citizens of the other; wherefore, all hostilities, both by sea and land, shall then immediately cease; all prisoners on both sides shall be set at liberty, and his Britannic Majesty shall, with all convenient speed, and without causing any destruction, or carrying away any negroes, or other property of the American inhabitants, withdraw all his armies, garrisons and fleets from the said United States, and from every port, place, and harbour within the same, leaving in all fortifications the American artillery that may be therein; and shall also order and cause all achieves, records, deeds, and papers, belonging to any of the said States, or their citizens, which in the course of the war, may have fallen into the hands of his officers, to be forthwith restored and delivered to the proper States and person to whom they belong.

AFTER PRELIMINARY ARTICLES WERE READ IN THE HOUSE OF
LORDS, EARL PEMBROKE MAKES A MOTION TO THANK THE KING
(EXTRACT ONLY) FOLLOWED BY LORD OSBORNE SECONDING THE
MOTION. SOME LORDS AGREED, OTHERS VIOLENTLY DISAGREED
(EXCERPTS)
February 18, 1783

The Earl of PEMBROKE rose, and expressed his hopes that their
Lordships would be of opinion with him that his Majesty's conduct, in
laying before them the Preliminaries of Peace, merited their grateful
approbation. Peace would relieve the kingdom from a load of taxes;
revive the old, and open new channels of commerce; restore harmony
and mutual affection between the subjects of Great Britain and the
United States of America; and contribute to promote the happiness and
establish the tranquility of Europe. He moved,
That an Humble Address be presented to his Majesty, to return his
Majesty the thanks of this House for his gracious condescention in ordering to be laid before us the Preliminary Articles of the different Treaties
which his Majesty has concluded, and to assure his Majesty that we have
considered them with that attention which so important a subject requires...
The Marquis of CARMARTHEN (Lord Osborne) seconded this motion.
He reminded their Lordships how earnestly the nation wished for peace,
and congratulated them on its happy accomplishment. The confederacy
that had been formed against England was dissolved. The nation was
eased of an intolerable and encreasing load of taxes. Trade would revive,
commerce would flourish more than it had ever done, and Great Britain,
pursuing the plans of wisdom, moderation, and peace, would still be one
of the first powers of Europe.
The Earl of CARLISLE considered the Preliminaries as injurious to
the interests, and derogatory to the honour of Great Britain. The conclusion of the Peace he admitted to be legal, as the Crown possessed
undoubtedly, the right of making peace or war. But though it was legal,
it was not in his opinion expedient...
Lord WALSINGHAM questioned the right of the Crown to dismember
the empire without the consent of Parliament; arraigned the cruelty and
injustice of abandoning the Loyalists, and our Indian allies; derided the
folly of the British Negotiator who had fixed the boundary between North
America and Britain; touched on the comparative strength of this with
that of other nations...
Lord STORMONT, having stated with great accuracy the question
before their Lordships, viz. Whether the Prelimiary Articles of Peace were
such as merited their applause, or deserved their disapprobation, considered them for his own part as injurious to the essential interests,
dangerous to the safety, derogatory to the honour of Great Britain, and
not warranted or justified by the situation of the war...
He adverted to the shameful ignorance, and simplicity, and folly, and
absurdity, that appeared in the Negotiation and Provisional Articles of
Peace between England and the United American States. What reason
could be given for sending out such a man as Mr. Oswald to treat with
the four American Commissioners? He was far overmatched by any one

of them; nor would any man compare him to Dr. Franklin, or Mr. Laurens, or any one of the Commissioners - *impar Congressa Archilli* - said his Lordship; for I am sure there was not one of them who was not an Archilles, compared with him. But it was not Mr. Oswald, he said, that he had to do with, but those who considered in him and employed him.

The first question that the British agent ought to have put to the American Commissioners was, whether they had full powers to conclude and agree upon a general amnesty and restitution of goods to all Loyalists, without exception? These were men whom Britain was bound in justice, and honour, and gratitude, and affection, and every tie, to provide for and protect. Yet, alas for England as well as them! they were made a part of the price of peace.- Those who were the best friends of Britain, were *conomine*, on that very account, excepted from the dulgence of Congress. Britain connives at the bloody sacrifice and seeks for a shameful retreat at the expence of her most valiant and faithful sons!...

His Lordship next turned his attention to the boundary line that had been agreed on by the American Commissioners, and that very extraordinary geographer and politician Mr. Richard Oswald. There was, prefixed to the articles of peace between England and America, a very pompous preamble, setting forth that those treaties were the best observed in which were reciprocal advantages. He was a long time at a loss to understand the meaning of those words, *reciprocal advantages*. But at last he discovered, that they meant only the advantage of America. For in return for the manifold concessions on our part, not one had been made on theirs.

The Earl of SHELBURNE said,....He confessed that he had not been able to obtain such a Peace as were to be wished for, nor was such a Peace to have been expected...He had indulged hopes, from the many professions of candour that had fallen from that Lordship's, on the subject of peace, about a month ago, that they would have quashed the voice of clamour, and been studious to promote harmony and unanimity.

MR. PITT COMMENTS ON PEACE IN HOUSE OF COMMONS (EXCERPTS)
February 19, 1783

Mr. T. PITT began the Debate by declaring he rose with an equal share of regret and satisfaction, in feeling that the day, which they had all so ardently looked for was arrived, when an end was put to a ruinous war, and they were restored to the blessings of Peace; regret, at the recollection of the sacrifices they had been obliged to make to obtain that blessing. Peace was what they all loved, and what mankind in general panted for; and yet, however desirous a nation might be of Peace before it was obtained, and however loudly it might have been called for by the united voice of the people, it generally happened that Peace, when concluded, became unpopular, and those, who made it, were in consequence the objects of much obloquy and clamour...When two nations went to war, the one of them was most likely to gain the ascendant, and whoever had the ascendant, had a right to expect concessions from the opposite party as the price of Peace. That was the light in which he wished Gentlemen to view our situation previous to the obtainment of that Peace, the articles of which were upon the Table. With this view of the matter, if any gentlemen should pronounce the present a bad peace, he would call upon those gentlemen to prove their assertions; it was a question, that must be decided by facts alone. Again, it would be fair to ask those who asserted it to be a bad Peace, Could you have made a better?...

GENERAL WASHINGTON'S ORDERS TO HIS TROOPS, (EXCERPTS), DATED HEADQUARTERS, APRIL 18, 1783
June 9, 1783

From *The Morning Post.*

The Commander in Chief orders the cessation of hostilities between the United States of America and the King of Great Britain, to be publicly proclaimed to-morrow at twelve o'clock, at the new building; and that the proclamation which will be communicated herewith be read to-morrow evening at the head of every regiment and corps of the army; after which the chaplains, with the several brigades, will render thanks to Almighty God for all his mercies, particularly for his over-ruling the wrath of man to his own glory, and causing the rage of war to cease among the nations.

Although the proclamation before alluded to extends only to the prohibition of hostilities, and not to the annunciation of a general peace, yet it must afford the most rational and sincere satisfaction to every benevolent mind, as it puts a period to a long and doubtful contest, stops the effusion of human blood, opens the prospect to a more splendid scene, and like another morning star, promises the approach of a brighter day than hath hitherto illuminated the Western hemisphere. On such a happy day, which is the harbinger of peace, a day which completes the eighth year of the war, it would be ingratitude not to rejoice; it would be insensibility not to participate in the general felicity...

EXTRACTS OF TWO LETTERS FROM NEW YORK GENTLEMEN OF CHARACTER AND FORTUNE (EXCERPTS), DATED APRIL 6, 1783
June 9, 1783

From the moment I saw the Commissioners letter to Washington, I had little hope that this country would be recovered. The mystery and secrecy that reigned in the proceedings on your side of the water heightened my suspicions. It was pretended that the influence of the Crown was too great, and was increasing.- A system was adopted to retrench that influence; the casting off the Colonies was one of the most effectual steps for the purpose; and, consequently, a part of the system. Still, however, I cherished some faint hope, and waited impatiently for the King's speech. I need not tell you that it confirmed me in the opinion that America was lost...Had the suppression of the rebellion, or the management of the negotiation with Congress, been committed to Sir Guy Carleton, instead of that wonderful negotiator Mr. Oswald, affairs would have assumed a very different aspect and for that very reason the management was not committed to the former...

The poor Loyalists are shamefully abandoned, and cast on the mercy of those who have no mercy for them. What right had Mr. Oswald to sign away your estate, and mine, and those of other Loyalists? Or what can any man, possessed of sentiments of justice and honour, think of a nation that could deliberately confirm so glaring a piece of iniquity and baseness?...

As soon as the February packet arrived, Sir Guy Carleton sent out dispatches to Congress. The treaty is now officially before them, and we are anxiously waiting for their decision upon it. It is probable they will graciously condescend to ratify it, and even to recommend the stipulation for the Loyalists to the several Assemblies; but for some time past, the Assemblies have paid just as much regard to the recommendations of Congress as suited them, or they judged proper, and no more...But supposing the Rebels should permit the Loyalists to repurchase, how can this be done by men who are reduced to beggary? and this is the condition of nineteen out of twenty among the Refugees. Unless therefore Government enables the Loyalists to purchase their estates, this privilege, if even admitted, is but a mockery of their distress...

Take the Provisional Treaty altogether - the grant of independency, and of territory, far beyond what the rebels ever expected, - the neglect of those who hazarded every thing for Government, add that after repeated calls from Government to step forth, and assurances of protection and support. It is certainly the most extraordinary that ever was made by any nation!...I must suppose that there are some stipulations in reserve for its friends; that as the definitive treaty with America is not yet concluded, the loyalists will be somehow secured, and this place held by the King's troops, till they are put in actual possession of their property. This last measure is what you should loudly contend for in England; for if this place is once abandoned, the loyalist cannot have any possible redress, whatever treatment they meet with...I shall only add, that if Britain means to have a commercial connection with this country, her interest is no less concerned than her reputation, in taking some care of those who have risked everything in her behalf. A large majority of the Americans are Loyalists; and although all have not lost their property, yet they have a sympathetic feeling for each other; and to see those consigned to ruin, who stood forth to assert their Sovereign's and their country's cause, can have no effect on the rest, nor produce any favourable sentiments towards Great Britain.

Peace has been proclaimed here this week; but the proclamation brought no peace to the poor Loyalists. Never was there so settled a gloom before on the countenance of the audience, on such an occasion. The multitude that attended was great - but no one hazza'd, or shewed any mark of joy or approbation, but the reverse. The Americans are now threatened with a terrible Indian war. All the tribes from the Gulph of Mexico to the Northern Lakes have determined to take up the hatchet, and retaliate the cruelties they have received from the Rebels. This is the most formidable combination of the Indian nation ever known on this continent. The withdrawing the French army, and divisions among the Loyalist, will prevent the latter from joining the French, as was the intention of many. The Loyalists, for the present, must bow under the yoke - there is no prospect of deliverance.

111

New York, dated April 26th.

I wrote to you by the last packet that sailed about a fortnight ago, since which nothing has happened, except that New York is filled with persons from different States. Some have come in about business, others to claim and get possession of their houses, in which they are much disappointed, as none of them will be given up till the army goes off, and that I believe will not be possible for some months. It is said General Carleton will first see the articles of the treaty complied with, which the different States seem averse to, especially that respecting the Refugees, as you will see by the enclosed New Jersey Newspaper, which I have sent that you may see with what *lenity* they intend treating those that are so unhappy as to be obliged to remain with their families.

A fleet now lies at the Hook bound to Nova Scotia, with a part of those that intend settling there. They consist of upwards of nine thousand souls on board; the next embarkation will be twice that number; and unless some of the American Acts are repealed before the troops leave us, almost every person must go there, or somewhere else. They are bitter beyond expression, and will not suffer a person to go into one of their States. Some few have tried it, but they have been stripped and beat unmercifully, and sent back. General Carleton goes next week to meet General Washington and Governor Clinton of this State, and no doubt will do every thing he can for us poor unfortunate Refugees; but I dread the time when the British troops leave us. As to any busines, I cannot think of it till times are more settled; and, unless they restore me my estate, I shall have nothing to subsist upon. My prospect at present, as well as that of thousands of others, is a very gloomy one, and sometimes gets quite the better of me; however, I must trust in him who alone has power to save.

A PETITION IN THE HOUSE OF LORDS FOR HELP TO LOYALISTS (EXCERPTS)
June 25, 1783

Lord JOHN CAVENDISH reminded the House that he had two days before presented a Petition from the Agents of the American Loyalists, and at the same time given notice, that he meant to move something upon it...At present, he conceived, no man would deny that it was utterly impossible to try what ought to be done towards the relief of those unfortunate and meritorious persons, who had undoubted claims on this country, and who had incurred considerable distress, in consequence of their loyal and laudable attachment to its cause. He meant therefore to institute a Commission for the purpose of enquiring who were the persons so entitled to relief, and he meant also to make it a part of the Bill, that the Commissioners should report the result of their enquiries early in the next sessions to that House, that they might see their way upon the business, and know the grounds of it, before they came to any parliamentary proceeding upon the subject. His Lordship said, a great deal would depend upon the United States, as every gentleman must be aware; and they, he trusted, would act liberally on the occasion, and by a generous determination to forget and forgive, lay the seeds of future confidence between the two countries. This, he flattered himself would be the case, because America must see the great value and importance of the friendship of Great Britain, and could not have to learn, that the closer connexion there was cemented between Great Britain and the United States, the more their mutual interest and their mutual strength would be promoted and established; But this must necessarily be a work of some little time. Passions, prejudices and resentment, would he hoped, die away on both sides, and good humour, regard, and confidence, encrease more and more. That being the case, he trusted by the time the Commissioners to be appointed under the new Bill, had gone the length of a report, Great Britain, and the United States would perfectly understand each other, and between them both, effectual relief would be administered to those, who had been distressed in consequence of the late unfortunate civil war. His Lordship concluded with moving, that the following paragraph of his Majesty's Speech, at the commencement of the Sessions be read:

"I have ordered enquiry to be made into the application of the sum voted in support of the American sufferers; and I trust that you will agree with me, that a due and generous attention ought to be shewn to those who have relinquished their properties or possessions from motives of loyalty to me, or attachment to the Mother Country."

This being done, he moved, for leave to bring in a Bill for the Institution of a commission to enquire into the distresses of all who have suffered in consequence of the American war.

GENERAL WASHINGTON'S CIRCULAR LETTER OF FAREWELL TO WM. GREENE, ESQ., GOVERNOR OF THE STATE OF RHODE ISLAND (EXCERPTS), DATED HEADQUARTERS, NEWBURGH, JUNE 18, 1783
August 12, 1783

The great object for which I had the honour to hold an appointment in the service of my country, being accomplished, I am now preparing to resign it into the hands of Congress, and return to that domestic retirement, which, it is well known, I left with the greatest reluctance; a retirement for which I have never ceased to sigh through a long and painful absence, in which (remote from the noise and trouble of the world) I mediate to pass the remainder of life, in a state of undisturbed repose; but, before I carry this resolution into effect, I think it a duty incumbent on me to make this my last official communication to congratulate you on the glorious events which Heaven has been pleased to produce in our favour, to offer my sentiments respecting some important subjects, which appear to me to be intimately connected with the tranquility of the United States, to take my leave of your Excellency as a public character, and to give my final Blessing to that country, in whose service I have spent the prime of my life; for whose sake I have consumed so many anxious days and watchful nights, and whose happiness, being extremely dear to me, will always constitute no inconsiderable part of my own...

There are four things which I humbly conceive are essential to the well-being, I may even venture to say, to the existence of the United States as an independent power.

1st. An indissoluble union of the States under one federal head.

2dly. A sacred regard to public justice.

3dly. The adoption of a proper peace establishment. And,

4thly. The prevalence of that pacific and friendly disposition among the people of the United States, which will induce them to forget their local prejudices and policies, to make those mutual concessions, which are requisite to the general prosperity, and, in some instances, to sacrifice their individual advantages to the interest of the community.

These are the pillars on which the glorious fabric of our independency and national character must be supported.- Liberty is the basis - and whoever would dare to sap the foundation, or overturn the structure, under whatever specious pretexts he may attempt it, will merit the bitterest execration, and the severest punishment, which can be inflicted by his injured country.

A LETTER FROM A GENTLEMAN IN ST. CROIX (EXCERPTS) FROM *FREEMAN'S NORTH AMERICAN JOURNAL*, PHILADELPHIA, JUNE 25, DATED MAY 24TH
August 13, 1783

"It is with the greatest satisfaction that I can now congratulate my friend on the happy return of the blessings of peace and the establishment of a glorious independence which I hope is on a basis that never will be shaken. It is an event that cannot but create joy in the heart of every true friend of liberty and America; an effect which I assure you it has not failed to produce among the Whigs of Santa Cruz who, though so far distant, have nevertheless felt for the sufferings of your country, and are equally elated with the success, and partake with real satisfaction in the rejoicings on the present glorious occasion. On the 19th of April a grand entertainment was given at Butler's bay to all the friends of America in the island, when the flag of the United States was displayed, and a vast number met to celebrate the day on which American blood was first shed in the cause of liberty and mankind. The Danish colours were likewise hoisted in compliment to the government, and afterwards the Irish and at daylight thirteen guns were fired to the honour of the United States. Inclosed you have a list of the toasts drunk on this occasion; his Danish Majesty's health was also drunk with a discharge of 21 cannons and to each of the other toasts thirteen. It is inconceivable how the Tories are mortified at the United States flag flying at Badlin and other harbours of our island. But why need I talk of Tories? You can scarcely meet with one now, they are all going to buy farms in America and settle in a country, which a few months ago they wished heartily for the destruction of; but I hope some good friends will have sagacity enough to discover those who have been most active against the United States, and have done their utmost to ruin and destroy such Americans as have fallen into their power, it will not be difficult to distinguish them, though they be ever so much disguised. Like Cain, they will always have some mark easy to be discovered.

LIST OF TOASTS

1. Congress, or the Thirteen United States of America: God prosper them with every blessing until time shall be no more.

2. The great, the illustrious Washington, the Father and Saviour of his country, who so nobly began, and so gloriously finished the work of our independence.- God bless him.

3. The great and illustrious kings, princes and states, who have been aiding and assisting the United States.

4. Benjamin Franklin, Esq. and the rest of the Ambassadors from the United States to the Court of France, who have so effectually settled the independence of America.

5. General Greene, and the other generals and soldiers, who have bravely fought for the liberties of their country.

6. The immortal memory of Warren and Montgomery, and those heroes who have fallen in the glorious cause of their country.

7. The rising navy of America, may they be more successful in their future marine operations than heretofore.

8. The Pennsylvania Farmer, and the virtuous governor of the United States.

9. May the American States exceed the republics of Sparta, Athens and Rome in public virtue, learning and military glory.

10. May liberty of conscience universally prevail in America, and may there be the asylumn of the distressed and oppressed from every part of the globe.

11. May friendship ever subsist between the subjects of Denmark and the free citizens of America for their mutual commercial interests.

12. The volunteers of Ireland, and the sons of freedom throughout the world.

13. Since Britain has seen her error, and returns with conciliating love, may all animosity be forgotten, and the independent States of America prove the prop and support of her old age.

A LETTER FROM CHARLESTOWN (EXCERPTS), DATED 1ST OF JULY
August 13, 1783

On the 16th ult, the sale of the confiscated estates began, according to advertisement, and a great many houses, land, &c. have been disposed of, at prices indicating the expected affluence of the haughty infant state.

It was thought a step of this important nature, would not have taken place, as by the Provisional Treaty, it is expressly agreed, and not made a matter of simple recommendation by Congress to the States, "That there shall be no future confiscations," which, on the idea of restitution, according to the spirit of the Treaty, must clearly relate to transfers of property, as the essential evil to be restrained, and not to new laws, which would only be the instruments of that evil. Indeed, the exiles have nothing left for the laws to operate upon, but debts, which are always exempted from confiscation in wars between civilised nations. However, this apparent difficulty has been surmounted by an explicit declaration, "that the Treaty cannot control the laws of the State;" So that on this principle, persons affected, being precluded by the late Act from recovering their debts, they likewise may be eventually confiscated by Taxes imposed on that species of property in the mean time, and the Provisional Treaty wholly eluded, unless the Definitive Treaty puts these matters to rights.

A LETTER FROM AN OFFICER AT NEW YORK TO HIS FRIEND IN EDINBURGH (EXTRACT), DATED JUNE 16TH
August 14, 1783

Congress have already passed resolves that we have infringed the treaty by allowing the negroes to go off, and have sent instructions to Dr. Franklin, at Paris, accordingly. It is true, we have sent above 800 to Nova Scotia, with 10,000 refugees; but Sir Guy Carleton very properly and humanly observes, that, as the faith of government was pledged to the negroes, he will not give them up, but if Commissioners hereafter to be appointed, shall determine that they ought to have been surrendered, Great Britain ought and must pay for them; for it would be the height of cruelty to deliver them up, as at least one half of them would be tortured to death. The different States or Assemblies have all passed resolves prohibiting the admission of the Loyalists, or returning any of their property; and some who have gone out from hence to visit their friends in the country, have been most cruelly treated. This has occasioned many more people to leave this country than otherwise would have done, as they are really afraid to stay. Upwards of 10,000 are already gone to different parts of Nova Scotia and I suppose as many more will still go there, to Canada, or the West Indies. The rebel army is all disbanded, excepting about 2,000 men; I ought rather to say, disunited, as they are only sent to their houses, and still are kept in pay, or the promise of it.

LORD MAYOR OF LONDON RECEIVES THE NEWS OF THE SIGNING OF THE PEACE TREATIES
September 8, 1783

St. James, Sept. 6
Thirty Minutes past Eleven, P.M.

My Lord,
I HAVE the honour to acquaint your Lordship, that Captain Warner is just arrived with the Preliminary Articles between his Majesty and the States General, signed at Paris on the second instant; as also the Definitive Treaties with France and Spain, signed at Versailles the third instant, by the Duke of Manchester, his Majesty's Ambassador extraordinary and Plenipotentiary, and the respective Plenipotentiaries of the said Courts and States;
The Definitive Treaty with the United States of America was also signed at Paris the third instant, by David Hartley, Esq. his Majesty's Plenipotentiary, and the Plenipotentiaries of those States, and will be brought over by Mr. Hartley himself.
I send your Lordship immediate notice of these important events, in order that they may be made publick in the City without loss of time.
C. J. Fox

A PRAISE OF BENJAMIN FRANKLIN
September 8, 1783

Doctor Franklin is incessantly occupied in preparing documents of different kinds on the prevailing circumstances of his native country. The finances, the civil polity, nay, each material object of municipal regulation, he takes the trouble to discuss at large; from time to time forwarding his reflections by the different vessels going to America.

At whatever passages in Dr. Franklin's public character party spirit may take occasion to cavil, candour must confess him to be highly praise worthy for the unabating zeal and consistent sagacity of his patriotism! What might not other powers have achieved, if they had been ministered to by such able and faithful servants?

THE FUTURE OF LOYALISTS
September 8, 1783

The investigations into the petitions of the respective Loyalists are to be conducted with a spirit of patience and impartial judgement, which has hitherto in all instances characterised the present ministry.

Respecting the future residence of the Loyalists, it appears to be the general expectation, as well as the general wish, that they will all add themselves to the mass of useful subjects in Great Britain.

By the friends of the families and individuals now unhappily in America, it is considered as a cause of no small satisfaction, that the removal of the troops from New York and other public intercourse between Great Britain and America, will afford sure opportunities to every man who chooses it, of returning to Europe.

WHAT IS HAPPENING IN GEORGIA?
September 8, 1783

The province of Georgia is almost depopulated. Most of the gentlemen of distinction and property there were Loyalists, and on the evacuation of the province by the King's troops, they left the country and carried off their negroes. Others of the Loyalists were cruelly murdered, for their attachment to the Sovereign. It is calculated, that not a tenth part of the white inhabitants, that were in Georgia at the breaking out of the civil war, remain there at this time, and the proportion of negroes is much less. The representatives of Georgia in former times used to vote themselves wages, but the whole taxes of the province, it is computed, are not now sufficient for that purpose; accordingly, Georgia is not now represented in Congress. What is to become of their Governor, and the numerous train of civil officers? Is government in Georgia to be dissolved? Or is the expence thereof to be devolved on the other United States?

117

A LETTER FROM A GENTLEMAN ON A TOUR TO PARIS TO HIS FRIEND IN LONDON REGARDING THE SIGNING OF THE PEACE TREATY (EXCERPTS)
September 12, 1783

As Mr. Warner, Secretary to our Ambassador at this Court, set off yesterday evening at three o'clock from Versailles, with the Definitive Treaty, which had been just signed...I am sorry that he does not carry with him the Commercial Treaty, which has been so long negotiating with America; but I can assure you, in the very words of Dr. Franklin, to a friend of mine, that the Commercial Treaty is vanished in smoke. What were the grounds on which the difference turned between England and America, and which prevented the conclusion of the treaty, is easy to discover; but some of them at least may be ascertained; though the British Ministers may not perhaps be very ready to avow them. Early in the negotiation, Dr. Franklin asked Mr. Hartley if any mention was made of Ireland in his instructions, and if he had any power to name, and specifically include, that kingdom in the treaty? Mr. Hartley did not seem prepared for such a question; he answered it however in the negative; Dr. Franklin upon this observed, that as Ireland was now avowedly an independent kingdom, it might hereafter be made a a question, how far she could be understood to be included without being named, in a treaty entered into by Great Britain...Mr. Hartley should write to his Court for instructions on this head. Whether the English Commissioner did so or not, you can learn better at home, than from me; but certain it is that Mr. Hartley never after mentioned one word upon the subject of Ireland to the American Minister; so that it is fair to conclude, either that he did not write a word about the business to his Court, which is excessively improbable, or that the Cabinet of St. James do not like the idea, and refused to comply with the Doctor's requisition; be that however as it may, you may rest assured that on Monday last the negotiation with America was at an end, and Mr. Hartley was preparing to return home.

...I forgot to mention that a Gentleman having waited upon Mr. Hartley to ask if Ireland was to be mentioned in the treaty, the Commissioner thought it a matter of such delicacy to speak on the subject, that he referred him for an answer to his Majesty's Ministers...there is something mysterious in the business, which may be hid till the opening of Parliament; and then a true opinion may be formed on the subject.

Yesterday was a Gala day at Versailles, in consequence of the signing of the Definitive Treaty; the Ministers of the different powers, who were parties to it, went in grand ceremony from hence to Versailles, and did not return till late in the evening. Mr. Warner however was dispatched from Versailles with the treaty, in a few minutes after it was signed.

WHERE WILL BE THE SEAT OF GOVERNMENT IN THE UNITED STATES?
September 13, 1783

Letters from Princetown say, that a disagreement prevails among the members of Congress, on the subject of determining where the seat of

Government shall be established; and it is added, that several of the members are warm advocates for meeting by rotation in each of the United States.

THE DEFINITIVE TREATY BETWEEN GREAT BRITAIN AND THE UNITED STATES IS SIGNED IN PARIS THE 3RD DAY OF SEPTEMBER, 1783
(listing Article I only)
September 30, 1783

IN THE NAME OF THE MOST HOLY AND UNDIVIDED TRINITY
It having pleased the divine Providence to dispose the Hearts of the Most Serene and Most Potent Prince George the Third, by the Grace of God, King of Great Britain, France and Ireland, Defender of the Faith, Duke of Brunswick and Lunenbourg, Arch-Treasurer, and Prince Elector of the Holy Roman Empire, &c. and of the United States of America, to forget all past Misunderstandings and Differences that have unhappily interrupted the good Correspondence and Friendship which they mutually wish to restore, and to establish such a beneficial and satisfactory Intercourse between the two Countries upon the Ground of reciprocal Advantages and mutual Convenience as may promote and secure to both perpetual Peace and Harmony; and having for this desirable End already laid the Foundation of Peace and Reconciliation by the Provisional Articles, signed at Paris on the 30th of November 1782, by the Commissioners empowered on each Part, which Articles were agreed to be inserted in, and to constitute the Treaty of Peace proposed to be concluded between the Crown of Great Britain and the said United States, but which Treaty was not to be concluded until terms of Peace should be agreed upon between Great Britain and France, and his Britannic Majesty should be ready to conclude such Treaty accordingly; and the Treaty between Great Britain and France having since been concluded, his Britannic Majesty and the United States of America in order to carry into full effect the Provisional Articles above mentioned, according to the Tenor thereof, have constituted and appointed, that is to say, his Britannic Majesty on his Part, David Hartley, Esq. Member of the Parliament of Great Britain, and the said United States on their Part, John Adams, Esq; late a Commissioner of the United States of America at the Court of Versailles, late Delegate in Congress from the State of Massachusetts and Chief Justice of the said State, and Minister Plenipotentiary of the said United States to their High Mightinesses the States General of the United Netherlands; Benjamin Franklin, Esq.; late Delegate in Congress from the State of Pennsylvania, President of the Convention of the said State and Minister Plenipotentiary from the United States of America at the Court of Versailles; and John Jay, Esq; late President of Congress and Chief Justice of the State of New York and Minister Plenipotentiary from the said United States at the Court of Madrid; to be the Plenipotentiaries for the concluding and signing the present Definitive Treaty;...after having reciprocally communicated their respective Full Powers, have agreed upon and confirmed the following Articles:

ARTICLE I

His Britannic Majesty acknowledges the said United States, viz. New Hampshire, Massachusetts Bay, Rhode Island and Providence Plantations, Connecticut, New York, New Jersey, Pennsylvania, Delaware, Maryland, Virginia, North Carolina, South Carolina and Georgia, to be free Sovereign and Independent States, that he treats with them as such, and for himself, his Heirs, and Successors, relinquishes all Claims to the Government, Propriety and Territorial Rights of the same and every Part thereof.

BRITISH MINISTERS -- 1763-1783

(As listed in *The American Revolution,* by Eric Robson, Senior Lecturer in History, University of Manchester, London, 1955.)

A Secretaryship of State for the Colonies (sometimes called the "American Department") was first created on February 27, 1768, and lapsed in March, 1782.

The office of First Lord of Trade and Plantations was suppressed in June 1782 and its business transferred to the Secretaries of State. In 1782, also, the Northern and Southern Departments were changed to Foreign Affairs and Home Affairs.

LORD CHANCELLOR

January 16, 1761	Lord Henley (later Earl of Northington)
July 30, 1766	Lord Camden
January 17, 1770	Charles Yorke
January 21, 1770	(In Commission)
January 23, 1771	Lord Apsley (Earl Bathurst; 1775)
June 3, 1778	Lord Thurlow
April 9, 1783	(In Commission)
December 23, 1783	Lord Thurlow

FIRST LORD OF THE TREASURY

May 28, 1762	Earl of Bute
April 15, 1763	George Grenville
July 10, 1765	Marquess of Rockingham
August 2, 1766	Duke of Grafton
February 5, 1770	Lord North
March 27, 1782	Marquess of Rockingham
July 13, 1782	Earl of Shelburne
April 4, 1783	Duke of Portland
December 27, 1783	William Pitt

CHANCELLOR OF THE EXCHEQUER

May 28, 1762	Sir Francis Dashwood
April 15th, 1763	George Grenville
July 10, 1765	William Dowdeswell
August 2, 1766	Charles Townshend
December 10, 1767	Lord North
March 27, 1782	Lord John Cavendish
July 13, 1782	William Pitt
April 4, 1783	Lord John Cavendish
December 27, 1783	William Pitt

SECRETARY OF STATE

	Northern	**Southern**
In office, 1762	Earl of Bute	Earl of Egremont
May 29, 1762	George Grenville	Earl of Egremont
October 14, 1762	Earl of Halifax	Earl of Egremont
September 9, 1763	Earl of Sandwich	Earl of Halifax
July 11, 1765	Duke of Grafton	Gen. H.S.Conway
May 24, 1766	Gen. H. S. Conway	Duke of Richmond
August 11, 1766	Gen. H. S. Conway	Earl of Shelburne
January 21, 1768	Viscount Weymouth	Earl of Shelburne
October 21, 1768	Earl of Rochford	Viscount Weymouth
December 20, 1770	Earl of Sandwich	Earl of Rochford
January 23, 1771	Earl of Halifax	Earl of Rochford
June 13, 1771	Earl of Suffolk	Earl of Rochford
November 11, 1775	Earl of Suffolk	Viscount Weymouth
October 28, 1779	Viscount Stormont	Viscount Weymouth
November 24, 1779	Viscount Stormont	Earl of Hillsborough

	Foreign Affairs	**Home Affairs**
March 27, 1782	Charles James Fox	Earl of Shelburne
July 19, 1782	Lord Grantham	Lord Sydney
April 2, 1783	Charles James Fox	Lord North
December 19, 1783	Earl Temple	----- -----
December 23, 1783	Lord Carmarthen	Lord Sydney

SECRETARY OF STATE FOR THE COLONIES

January 21, 1768	Earl of Hillsborough
August 14, 1772	Earl of Dartmouth
November 11, 1775	Lord George Germaine
February 11, 1782	Welbore Ellis

FIRST LORD OF THE ADMIRALTY

January 1, 1763	George Grenville
April 23, 1763	Earl of Sandwich
September 10, 1763	Earl of Egmont
September 10, 1766	Sir Charles Saunders
December 10, 1766	Sir Edward Hawke
January 12, 1771	Earl of Sandwich
March 30, 1782	Viscount Keppel
January 28, 1783	Viscount Howe
April 8, 1783	Viscount Keppel
December 30, 1783	Viscount Howe

FIRST LORD OF TRADE AND PLANTATIONS

March 1, 1763	Charles Townshend
April 20, 1763	Earl of Shelburne
September 9, 1763	Earl of Hillsborough
July 20, 1765	Earl of Dartmouth
August 16, 1766	Earl of Hillsborough
December 1766	Robert Nugent (later Viscount Clare and Earl Nugent)
January 20, 1768	Earl of Hillsborough
August 14, 1772	Earl of Dartmouth
November 10, 1775	Lord George Germaine
November 6, 1779	Earl of Carlisle
December 9, 1780	Lord Grantham

SECRETARY OF WAR

March 18, 1761	Charles Townshend
December 17, 1762	Welbore Ellis
July 17, 1765	Viscount Barrington
December 16, 1778	Charles Jenkinson
March 27, 1782	Thomas Townshend (later Viscount Sydney)
July 11, 1782	Sir George Yonge
April 11, 1783	Richard Fitzpatrick
December 24, 1783	Sir George Yonge

NOTES - CHAPTER I

(1) P. 1 - Jarrett, *Britain 1688-1815*, p. 297

(2) P. 1 - Jarrett, *Britain 1688-1815*, p. 297

(3) P. 2 - Heale, *The American Revolution*, p. 7

(4) P. 3 - Pemberton, *Lord North*, p. 214

(5) P. 3 - Guedalla, *Independence Day*, p. 40

(6) P. 3 - Egerton, *The American Revolution*, p. 101

(7) P. 4 - Pemberton, *Lord North*, p. 197

(8) P. 4 - Pemberton, *Lord North*, p. 197

NOTES - CHAPTER II

(1) P. 5 - Guedalla, *Independence Day*, p. 39

(2) P. 6 - Pemberton, *Lord North*, p. 264

(3) P. 6 - Pemberton, *Lord North*, p. 264

(4) P. 6 - Nevins & Commager, *America*, p. 80

(5) P. 6 - Wrong, *Washington and His Comrades*, p. 68

(6) P. 7 - Wrong, *Washington and His Comrades*, p. 129

(7) P. 7 - Egerton, *The American Revolution*, p. 122

(8) P. 7 - Wrong, *Washington and His Comrades*, p. 130

(9) P. 8 - Robson, *The American Revolution*, p. 177

(10) P. 8 - Robson, *The American Revolution*, p. 180

(11) P. 8 - Robson, *The American Revolution*, p. 181-182

(12) P. 8 - Robson, *The American Revolution*, p. 187

(13) P. 8 - Robson, *The American Revolution*, p. 191

(14) P. 8 - Egerton, *The American Revolution*, p. 140

BIBLIOGRAPHY

Adams, James Truslow. *The Epic of America.* London, 1943.

Egerton, H.E. *The Causes and Character of the American Revolution.* Oxford, 1923.

Guedalla, Philip. *Independence Day.* London, 1926.

Heale, M. J. *The American Revolution.* London, 1986.

Jarrett, Derek. *Britain 1688-1815.* London, 1965.

Lecky, William Edward Hartpole. *History of England in the Eighteenth Century, Vol. III.* New York, 1882.

Mayo, Katherine. *General Washington's Dilemna.* London, 1938.

Nevins, Allan and Commager, Henry Steele. *America - The Story of a Free People.* Oxford, 1942.

Pemberton, W. Baring. *Lord North.* London, 1938.

Robson, Eric. *The American Revolution in its Political and Military Aspects.* London, 1955.

Smith, T. C. *The Wars Between England and America.* London, 1914/15.

Times, The And Barclays Bank. *1776 The British Story of the American Revolution.* National Maritime Museum, London, 1976.

Wright, Esmond. *Washington and the American Revolution.* Harmondsworth, 1957.

Wrong, George M. *Washington and His Comrades in Arms.* Oxford, 1921.

129

CORBIN, Edmund 59
CORNWALLIS, 13 21 22 30
  34-36 48 49 62 63 69
  70 72 Charles Earl 30
  34 Earl 14 29 64 70
  77 87 Lord 13 14 21
  22 26-32 34 50-52 54
  55 63 66-70 72 73 77-
  79 82 83 87
DASHWOOD, Francis 122
DEANE, 8 Silas 7
DEGALVEZ, Don Bern 58
DEGRASSE, Count 64 70
  Monsieur 87
DELAFAYETTE, Marquis 6
  12 73
DEROCHAMBAULT, Count 13
DEROCHAMBEAU, Compte 99
  Count 22 23 64 69
DESTAING, Compte 9
  Monsieur 32
DIGBY, 62 Adm 60 62 92
  Rear Adm 60 62
DOWDESWELL, William 122
DUKE OF BRUNSWICK, 119
DUKE OF CHANDOS, 77 78
  87
DUKE OF GRAFTON, 78 121
  122
DUKE OF LUNENBOURG, 119
DUKE OF MANCHESTER, 75
  78 116
DUKE OF PORTLAND, 121
DUKE OF RICHMOND, 65
  74-76 78 122
DUNDAS, Charles 53
EARL OF BUTE, 121 122
EARL OF CARLISLE, 108
  123
EARL OF CHATHAM, 53
EARL OF CORNWALLIS, 87
EARL OF DARTMOUTH, 122
  123
EARL OF EGMONT, 123
EARL OF EGREMONT, 122
EARL OF HALIFAX, 122
EARL OF HILLSBOROUGH,
  122 123
EARL OF LINCOLN, 14
EARL OF NORTHINGTON,
  121

EARL OF PEMBROKE, 108
EARL OF ROCHFORD, 122
EARL OF SANDWICH, 122
  123
EARL OF SHELBURNE, 103
  109 121 122 123
EARL OF SUFFOLK, 122
EARL, William 93
EDWARDS, Stephen 97
ELLIOT, Edward James 93
ELLIS, Mr Secretary
  Welbore 27 122 123
ENGLISH COMMISSIONER,
  118
FIRST LORD OF THE
  ADMIRALTY, 123
FIRST LORD OF TRADE AND
  PLANTATIONS, 123
FIRST LORD OF TREASURY,
  121
FITZPATRICK, Mr 25
  Richard 123
FOX, C J 116 Charles
  James 122 Mr 27 49 50
  52-54 66 89 103
FRANKLIN, 8 11 Benjamin
  7 98 107 115 117 119
  Dr 19 56 61 99 109
  116-118
FRANKS, Maj 40
FURMAN, Gen 97
GAGE, Gen 5 Gen Thomas
  3 Thomas 5
GATES, 20 Gen 4 7 21 28
GEORGE, Lord 52, Sir 52
GEORGE III, King Of
  England 2 3 5 8
GEORGE III, Prince of
  England 119
GERMAIN, 7 15 48 60 G
  21 George 6 14 52 68
  Lord 8 14
GERMAINE, 6 George 122
  123
GIBBON, Mr 67
GORDON, Brig Gen 72
GOULD, Col 77
GOV OF GEORGIA, 117
GOV OF NEW YORK, 13
GOWER, Lord 78
GRANTHAM, Lord 122 123

SANDWICH, Earl 4th 6
SAUNDERS, Charles 123
SAVITZ, George 52
SCARSDALE, Lord 83
SCOTT, 13
SEC OF STATE, 122
SEC OF STATE FOR COLO-
NIES, 122
SEC OF WAR, 123
SECS OF STATE, 21
SHELBURN, Lord 91
SHELBURNE, Lord 75 76
78
SHELDON, Col 39
SMITH, Gen 27 Joshua 40
SOUTHHAMPTON, Lord 65
SPEAKER, Mr 79 81
STORMONT, 21 Lord 108
Viscount 122
STURMONT, Lord 78
SULLIVAN, John 46
SUMPTER, Brig Gen 34
Gen 28 34
SYDNEY, Lord 122 Vis-
count 123
SYMONDS, Thomas 64
TARLETON, Col 27 28 Lt
Col 14 34 48 49
TEMPLE, Earl 122
THOMPSON, Charles 42
102
THURLOW, Lord 121

TILTON, Capt 97 Clayton 97
TOWNSEND, Charles 3 Lord 83
Mr 51 66 Mr Sec 106
TOWNSHEND, Charles 122
123 Thomas 93 123
VARRICK, Col 40
WALKER, John 59
WALSINGHAM, Lord 108
WARNER, Capt 116 Mr 118
WARREN, 115
WASHINGTON, 6 11 16 37
57 58 62 69 70 110
115 G 17 38 92 Gen 5
6 12 17 22 37-43 55
63 64 92 95 105 110
112 113 George 5-7 11
96 97 Mr 18 55 70
WEBSTER, Lt Col 49
WEMYSS, Maj 106
WESTCOTE, Lord 50 51
WEYMOUTH, Viscount 122
Viscount 3rd 6
WHITCOMB, Lt 72
WHITE, Philip 97
WILKES, Alderman 30 31
Mr 31
WRAXALL, Mr 46 47
WYCOMB, Lord 65
Y---G, 59
YONGE, George 94 123
YORKE, Charles 121

www.ingramcontent.com/pod-product-compliance
Lightning Source LLC
Chambersburg PA
CBHW070451090426
42735CB00012B/2512